D1615389

STRANGE INTELLIGENCE

From Dunkirk to Nuremberg

STRANGE INTELLIGENCE

From Dunkirk to Nuremberg

S. JOHN PESKETT

ROBERT HALE · LONDON

© S. John Peskett 1981
First published in Great Britain 1981

ISBN 0 7091 8978 8

Robert Hale Limited
Clerkenwell House
Clerkenwell Green
London EC1R 0HT

Photoset by
Specialised Offset Services Limited, Liverpool
and printed in Great Britain by
Lowe & Brydone Ltd., Thetford, Norfolk
Bound by Weatherby Woolnough Ltd., Northants.

Say, from whence
You owe this strange intelligence?

Macbeth, I, iii

Contents

Illustrations

PICTURE CREDITS

The author thanks the following for permission to reproduce pictures: Imperial War Museum (1–5, 7); U.S. Signal Corps (20–23).

Acknowledgements

I should like to express my thanks to the Ministry of Defence (Air Historical Branch) for encouragement in the writing of this book which, while not claiming to be more than an account of personal experiences, may add to the official record some unusual aspects of intelligence work in the last war. I am also grateful to Sir Hugh Greene and Professor R.V. Jones for reading those parts of the book relevant to their war-time association with some of the activities described, though I must point out that the views expressed are entirely my own.

Finally I am greatly indebted to Peter Endsleigh Castle not only for designing the jacket and drawing the map but for much helpful advice and recollections of the war years when we were working together.

Maudite, en haine aux mères, tenue pour fléau de Dieu, depuis que la guerre est guerre elle engendre chez ceux qui l'ont faite, sitôt passée, le sentiment le plus inattendu: la nostalgie.

Dominique Aury in her preface to
Servitude et Grandeur Militaires
of Alfred de Vigny

Ever since war has existed, it has been cursed, hated by mothers and seen as the scourge of God; yet in all those who have made war, there is engendered, once it is over, the most unexpected sentiment — nostalgia.

Introduction

In 1939 I was granted a commission in the Administrative and Special Duties Branch of the Royal Air Force. It proved to be a roving commission with the accent on special duties. As an Air Staff intelligence officer for seven years, I found myself called upon to do a variety of unusual jobs which I had never associated with the Royal Air Force; from sitting in a trench in the Maginot Line to carrying out inquests on innumerable shot-down enemy aircraft, interrogating prisoners of war, working on the Ultra Secret at Bletchley Park, broadcasting propaganda to the Luftwaffe, training officers for the government of Germany and interviewing one of the major war criminals at Nuremberg.

To the albatross, serenely soaring through the blue vault of heaven, that poor solitary speck on the ice down there is a pitiful sight. It is a humble penguin. The unhappy flightless creature, with feet firmly planted, cocks up a beady eye and sees the magnificent spectacle of the apparently effortless conquest of space and gravity. Thus nature gives grace and beauty with one hand and with the other fixes the uncomely penguin securely to the ground.

In any air force every man in the air, whether in fighters or bombers, reconnaissance or transport aircraft, is held up not only by the lift in the wings of his machine but by a pyramid of men who stay on terra firma. Beginning with the boffins who design aircraft and think up gadgets, the ground crews, plotters, armourers, radio and radar operators, doctors, cooks, observers, meteorologists, intelligence officers and many others, all play their part in keeping him up there. They see that the flying man is properly trained, fit, well equipped and correctly informed about the enemy. They ensure that his aircraft and everything he uses are thoroughly serviced and that his safety is assured as far as possible.

Many of these jobs receive little acclaim beside that of the man who does the fighting in the air. Yet one flaw in one link of this chain of ancillary ground activities puts his life in jeopardy as well as the operation on which he is engaged.

This is the story of my roving commission and an account of the work of one branch of flightless birds, which, it is hoped, made some contribution towards the achievements of the men of the Royal Air Force who flew in the last war, so many of whom did not live to see the end of it as we did. It is to them that this book is dedicated.

PART I

The End in France

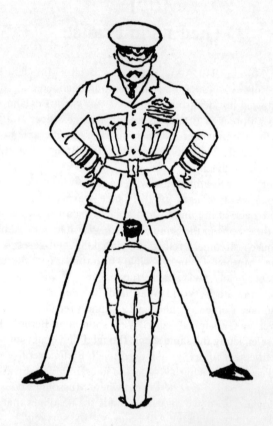

First encounter with the Commander-in-Chief

I

On 18th March 1940 Adolf Hitler and Benito Mussolini met at the Brenner railway station. This momentous encounter to some extent overshadowed my departure that same day from England to join the British Air Forces in France as an intelligence officer attached to the staff of the Commander-in-Chief. In fact considerable secrecy was observed regarding my journey, while the Brenner rendezvous was given headline publicity.

It all began at Southampton with an almost hopeless search for the craft which was to convey me to France. I expected a giant transport and at the back of my mind I had a vague picture of a heroic send-off such as the troops in the South African War had, with bands playing and coloured streamers reluctantly breaking and severing our bond with the Mother Country while beautiful girls fluttered white handkerchiefs and held back their tears. I was old enough to remember the First World War and the departure of the British Expeditionary Force to France in 1914 and I recalled the cries of "It'll all be over by Christmas!" and "We'll soon be in Berlin!" Here was I in 1940 re-enacting the same scene, though I had doubts about being in Berlin in the near future. I did indeed reach Berlin over five years later. I walked over Hitler's burial place and later, in Milan, I was shown the petrol station in the Piazzale Loreto where Mussolini's body was hung upside down. Those two may have made the headlines that day but in the end I could say with the Abbé Sieyès, "J'ai survécu!"

Acting on the vaguest of instructions from the embarkation office a small group of us finally located a venerable tub known to Lloyd's as the *Tynwald*. It looked as ancient as its name. My fellow passengers were mainly Army and other Royal Air Force officers and men returning from leave or, like myself, going out for the first time.

It can now be disclosed that the *Tynwald* was bound for Le Havre, which we reached after eighteen hours of sleeping, eating and reading

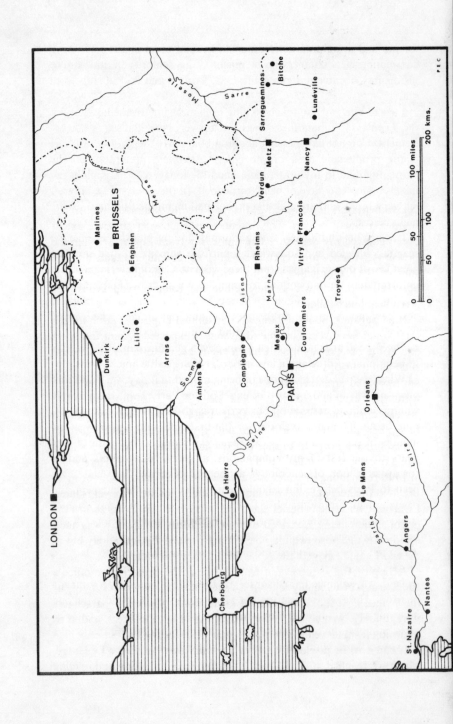

for me and a nightmare of confusion heaped upon chaos for a wing commander accountant, who by reason of his seniority in rank and to his dismay became automatically O.C. Troops and had to sort us all out.

I asked why we had taken so long even allowing for the antiquity of the *Tynwald*. "Submarines!" was the answer. Now the sea is not my element. I do not like messing about in boats. My idea of ocean travel is the promenade deck of the *Queen Elizabeth* preferably on the Serpentine and to my un-nautical mind the longer you stay afloat the more chance you have of being torpedoed. In the safety of Le Havre I felt very brave and grateful that no one had mentioned submarines the night before.

It was a delightful early spring morning and the sun shone while the seagulls wheeled and squawked round the ship as we tied up. The great joy of our arrival was that there were no Customs formalities but unfortunately we had nothing to smuggle. We all crowded into the big building of the Compagnie Générale Transatlantique and spent the next few hours in the large hall changing our money into francs, buying food, drink and papers and writing our first "On Active Service" postcards home. I felt I was now a genuine part of the British Expeditionary Force and a link in our far-flung battle line.

When we had given up hope of being moved that day, we heard that our train was in and a crowd of us set off for Paris. I was the only one with no ultimate destination but Paris was good enough for me for the time being. Though I was out for the first time and had only a few months of service in the R.A.F., I felt very senior with my thirty-four years to the rest of my companions, all very young pilots and as rowdy as a mob of schoolboys at the end of term. They had never been to Paris before, but I could remember my own excitement and bewilderment on my first visit to Paris seventeen years earlier, when I stood outside a café in the rue d'Amsterdam at six o'clock in the morning trying to explain to a sleepy waiter what an English breakfast was. I felt very experienced and handed out fatherly advice to all.

At last we arrived and, having collected all our bags on a big trolley, we advanced in disorder to the railway transport officer's quarters. Here we were sorted out again but I was once more the odd man out and still had no idea where I was to go, beyond the Gare de l'Est. Some of the others were due to depart thence, so we made up a convoy of taxis with camp kits perilously balanced on the roofs and set off.

At the Gare de l'Est I took leave of the young pilots and faced the world alone. The R.T.O. told me that H.Q., B.A.F.F. was to be found at Coulommiers, about an hour and a half to the east of Paris, and that I had about three hours to wait for the train. So I set off to look at Paris in wartime.

I have lived and travelled in sixty-four countries and in all the continents but my first venture into foreign parts was to Paris and it remains my first and last love. I learned to speak French at an early age and I have always felt more at home in France than in any other foreign country. Shortly after the 1914 war, I lodged in a poor quarter of Paris with a demobilized soldier and his wife, who were working as concierges of what was known as an hotel but was really a tenement. I came to know all the local characters through my landlord, who delighted in teaching me the foulest language of the trenches and encouraging me to drink vast quantities of *pinard*. This red wine was cheap enough for my impoverished host to buy half a dozen bottles a day.

Starting from the Hôtel Rival I discovered Paris, mostly on foot. From the place Félix-Faure I would plod up the avenue de la Motte Picquet into the boulevard de La Tour Maubourg to the Pont des Invalides and then follow the Seine eastwards. On my day-long walks I found out far more about the city than all the literary Americans who adopted Paris as their spiritual home – who wouldn't if one came from Arkansas or some such place? – and who spent their time sitting in cafés on the Left Bank talking about themselves to other Americans. On such promenades it is surprising what strange encounters one has and how many odd people one gets to know. Their French was not the French I heard at my lectures or at the law courts, which incidentally is one of the best places, apart from the national theatres, for learning how French should be spoken. Harold Nicolson once wrote: "It is impossible to use French correctly without being obliged to place one's ideas in the proper order, to develop them in a logical sequence, and to use words of almost geometrical accuracy." After the war, in a career in diplomacy, I found this to be very true, though Harold Nicolson makes it sound a coldly logical means of communication. I should like to add that it is not only the useful language of the diplomatist but the voice of Racine, of Molière, of Madame de Sévigné, of Flaubert, of Proust and, if you like, of Simenon. It is the language of *Le Grand Meaulnes* and *Zazie dans le Métro*. Yet in delighting in the infinite variety of French I do not forget that we can be proud to speak the language of Shakespeare and Milton. I am merely trying to transmit my enthusiasm for the French language and the way of life of which it is the expression. I cannot claim the degree of perfection in Harold Nicolson's definition but at least it was my knowledge of French, gained over many years and from the varied sources I have mentioned, which deposited me at the Gare de l'Est that day in March 1940.

I wondered how I was going to see all I wanted to see in three hours. I felt conspicuous in my new R.A.F. uniform as I set off down the boulevard de Strasbourg and turned right into the Grands Boulevards. There were many other uniforms of all kinds and ABRI signs here and there but Paris seemed otherwise little changed. A French soldier saluted me to my great surprise and this made me feel rather less lonely. I browsed in bookshops and promised myself an orgy of book-buying along the *quais* if I managed to get to Paris again. I took tea among the portly dowagers and *jeunes mariées* at the Café de la Paix and then made my way back to the station, where I loaded my baggage on to the train for Coulommiers.

The train stopped at every little station. One was called Mortcerf and another Crèvecoeur, which was far from cheering. By this time I realized that the black-out in France was blue. All lamps and window panes were painted dark blue so that one moved in a kind of submarine atmosphere. At Coulommiers I fully expected to have to spend the night in the railway station. However, there was a utility van awaiting me. The driver piled my luggage into the back and off we went through the darkness.

I learned from my driver that I was destined for No. 2 Mess in "the Château". Arrived at the entrance hall of what was an ordinary middle-class house, I was told that everyone was at dinner. This filled me with stage fright. It is one thing to slip into the ante-room of a mess and to mingle unobtrusively like a detective at a wedding, but it is a different ordeal altogether to appear before a full mess assembled at table. The mess secretary came out, a very fierce-looking flight lieutenant with a bristling moustache and a lame leg. He afterwards proved to be the kindest of people but he looked most forbidding then. He asked for my name and rank in a roaring voice and hauled me from the semi-darkness of the hall into the dining-room. I made my bow to the P.M.C. feeling rather like Burns's mouse turned up by the plough and sat down hastily and thankfully in the only vacant chair, next to my refuge and strength, the fierce flight lieutenant.

I was examined by all with slight interest and allowed to eat my dinner in peace. Only now and again did my neighbour, the flight lieutenant, bellow a remark intended to make me feel at home. Such efforts only served to terrify me. I made such replies as courtesy demanded and in a still small voice. Usually I am an aggressive and talkative character but this was scarcely an encouraging audience with a lot of top brass at one end of the table. It had a reputation as a "sticky" mess where conversation was not welcomed, especially from junior officers.

However, after dinner the atmosphere became more cordial. The air commodore asked me to have a drink and the wing commander insisted on lending me his eiderdown. The flight lieutenant mess secretary arranged for me to sleep in "The Annexe", another house opposite, and a flying officer conducted me to my room. It was quite empty and for the first time I felt glad I had brought my very cumbersome camp kit with me. After much unstrapping of strange-looking packages and with the advice of officers who had solid and comfortable beds, I erected my camp bed, my camp chair, my camp table and my camp wash-basin, all in tough green canvas. I then retired for the night under the wing commander's eiderdown. I discovered that, however much you have over you on a camp bed, you are always cold underneath.

II

Coulommiers is a little town of five or six thousand inhabitants on the Grand-Morin in the Brie cheese country. The town centre is a large square market place, from which cobbled streets lead in all directions. The rather opaque river winds its way through the town. Just off the market place is the church of Saint-Denis, built between the thirteenth and sixteenth centuries. It is a somewhat pitiful edifice and, as far as I could see, was used as a vegetable store. There was a tablet on the outside wall commemorating the fact that Joan of Arc passed through Coulommiers on one occasion. A little way off is the modern church, a large ugly building before which stands a heroic statue of Beaurepaire. He was commandant at Verdun in 1792 and he killed himself rather than surrender the town. It is a pity we had no Beaurepaire in 1940 – but I anticipate.

After a silent breakfast at No. 2 Mess, I was taken to Intelligence H.Q. about ten minutes away in the avenue de la Ferté-sous-Jouarre. Intelligence was lodged in one big house standing alone in a very neglected garden. A larger house on the opposite side of the avenue was pointed out to me with awe as the working quarters of the Commander-in-Chief, Air Marshal Barratt later Air Chief Marshal Sir Arthur Barratt.

The Intelligence H.Q. house was even more dilapidated inside than out. The room which I was to share with two or three other officers was bare except for two trestle tables and a few chairs. Our room was the antechamber to an "ops. room", where a large map on the wall bristled with coloured pins, flags and arrows. A small room opening from the other side of our room housed a wing commander who knew no French but was an expert in Arabic and Persian. Upstairs a number of R.A.F. clerks banged typewriters and built up a store of files. The group captain also had an office on the first floor. On the top floor lived the "Met" staff, whose predictions on the weather were received with incredulous ribaldry.

For some months before going to France I had been on the staff of A.C.A.S.(I), which is short for Assistant Chief of Air Staff (Intelligence), with the job of examining crashed or shot-down enemy aircraft. We started the war with a nucleus of about a dozen officers who had some technical or scientific experience. Some of us spoke German. We had to learn the work as we went along and as more and more enemy material fell into our hands. At first, shot-down enemy aircraft were fairly rare in the United Kingdom until the time of the Battle of Britain, when we had enough to fill several junk yards.

A shot-down or force-landed enemy aircraft is obviously a source of most valuable intelligence. It is of the greatest tactical, scientific, technical and industrial interest. The Air Ministry had priority in the handling of such aircraft. They were usually roped off by the local police and provided with a military guard until one of us arrived to make the preliminary report. Dead members of the crew or any survivors were dealt with by another branch of Air Intelligence. They had often been removed either to a local mortuary or to an interrogation centre by the time we appeared on the scene. If we arrived promptly we might find bodies still on board or scattered round the wreckage. I remember a Messerschmitt 110 twin-engine fighter which I had to examine near Enfield after I returned from France. It had been shot down by fighters and had made a belly landing among some greenhouses. In Luftwaffe slang a crash was referred to as a *Klavier aus dem fünften Stock*, which means a piano falling from the fifth floor. It must have sounded rather like that when this aircraft landed among the greenhouses. The petrol tanks had exploded and the aircraft was partly burnt out. The dead crew of two had not been removed. One was sitting about a hundred yards in front of the nose of the aircraft on the ground as if he had been resting. He appeared quite uninjured and was wearing his full flying kit. It was difficult to believe that he was dead. The other member of the crew was still in his seat, stark naked and roasted all over. The first time I found a dead man on an aircraft – he had had his head torn off – I was profoundly shocked and could not get it out of my mind for days afterwards, but fortunately, or perhaps unfortunately, one gets hardened. In England it was the duty of the interrogating officer to go through the pockets of the dead but I myself had to do it occasionally in France. Though aircrews on both sides were not supposed to carry anything on operations, which might give useful information to the enemy, we frequently found bus tickets, restaurant bills, photos and material of that kind. These could give a clue to the location of the man's unit or the transfer of a squadron. There would usually be a snapshot or two of the man's wife and children or his parents or girlfriend very much like the snapshots we had in our own wallets.

There were good reasons for giving us absolute priority apart from the protection of the aircraft as a source of intelligence material. Many shot-down aircraft still had bombs on board, machine guns and cannon which could go off at the pressure on a button and self-destroying devices which were fitted under the seats of fighter pilots. The latter was an explosive with a short delay which the pilot could operate if he force-landed and the aircraft was still intact. Bombs were not as dangerous as they might appear. German bombs were not armed until they left the aircraft, when a wiper switch operated automatically. One other danger we had to guard against was the souvenir hunter. I have rarely examined an enemy aircraft from which the clock had not been stolen. Often it was also the repeater compass on the dashboard which had mysteriously disappeared. The master compass was in the tail and much more difficult to get at. Finally there was the enthusiast who could not keep his hands off switches and knobs just to see how they worked. On one occasion a German bomber, a Heinkel 111, had landed with its bombs intact in their vertical bays. While I was doing my report a squadron leader from a near-by R.A.F. station came over to have a look. In the cockpit above the pilot's seat he noticed a handle, painted red and marked *Notzug für Bomben* (Emergency Release for Bombs). It was too much of a temptation. He pulled it. By the grace of God and thanks to the inventor of the wiper switch arming device, the aircraft was not blown up. The aircraft was lying on its belly with about a foot clearance off the ground where the bomb bays were located. The eight bombs all fell a foot, mercifully unarmed.

Even the preliminary examination of an enemy aircraft was quite a lengthy job. More detailed examinations and tests would be carried out later by the Royal Aircraft Establishment at Farnborough and other bodies specializing in bombs, mines, guns and so on. Of immediate importance were such items as identification of the unit and where it came from. Next any new type of armament or different location of armament or armour protection together with arcs of fire of the guns had to be reported at once for the benefit of our own fighters. If possible the cause of the crash had to be ascertained.

Sometimes we had both Fighter Command and the A.A. gunners waiting to know who could claim the credit. Engines, petrol, oil, radio, radar, bombsights and other instruments, quantity and type of ammunition, de-icing equipment and any novel features such as balloon-cable cutters had to be investigated and recommendations for further examinations made. Later the local R.A.F. Maintenance Unit would come and collect the wreck for disposal in accordance with our findings. On occasions almost intact aircraft were taken to Farnborough, repaired and given test flights. We once had a lucky find in a Junkers 88 servicing handbook on one aircraft. The translation of this into English was quite a task but it proved most useful to the R.A.F. ground personnel who were being trained to service German aircraft.

By March 1940 a number of enemy aircraft had been shot down over France and thus I found myself at Coulommiers as an Enemy Crash Intelligence Officer, the sole specimen of my kind outside the United Kingdom and with more enthusiasm than experience. The experience was to come rapidly and in quantity. The one advantage I had was that I had no master. With my driver I was an independent mobile unit free to go anywhere in France with the full support of the Royal Air Force and the blessing of the French Armée de l'Air. As long as I sent in my reports on crashed aircraft and any other information I managed to pick up in my peregrinations to H.Q. and thence to the Air Ministry in London, no one bothered me or kept me to a time-table and everyone from the top brass downwards gave me every possible help.

The French armed forces naturally had priority in the examination and disposal of enemy aircraft on French soil. This meant that I had to do a liaison job with the Deuxième Bureau (Intelligence) of the French Air Force, which was not far away at Saint-Jean-les-Deux-Jumeaux. Who the twins were I never found out. Wherever I went in France I had the help of the Deuxième Bureau and of all units of the French Army and Air Force. Apart from allowing me to examine "tout avion ennemi abattu", as my permit stated, I was allowed access to prisoners, I was fed and housed and filled up with petrol and red wine at every stop.

Those of us who had travelled in Germany before 1939 had seen that war was inevitable. I was so sure myself that I had put my name down early in that year and was called up as soon as war was declared. Though so many of us knew that there would be a war, we hardly imagined the kind of war we would have on our hands in France. Even less did we think that we would be sitting out month after month of fairly peaceful existence while enormous German forces stood poised on the other side of the frontier. I suppose we felt relieved that we could enjoy the spring and early summer in the pleasant French countryside, sleeping and eating as if we were at home instead of crouching in trenches or charging to death on the enemy barbed wire as in the First World War.

On looking back over forty years I feel far more frightened now than I did in 1940 even though at times I was uncomfortably close to the frontier. At any moment the Germans could throw in forces which could drive us into the sea and reduce the French, Belgian and Dutch armies to a standstill. Yet we went on with our daily routine, sleeping in comfortable beds and keeping peace-time hours. I travelled all over northern and eastern France doing my job. In addition I had time to do some sightseeing and to appreciate French cooking and some very fine wines. Panther, one of the outposts of the R.A.F., was at Rheims and there was no shortage of champagne. It was only after 10th May that life became difficult.

There was a fair amount of activity in the various French headquarters to which I was attached but, as far as the troops were concerned, one sensed a certain *je m'en foutisme*. In the Maginot Line in the evacuated towns and villages soldiers, even sentries, slouched around with their hands in their pockets. Some even wore carpet slippers. There was little of the "Ils ne passeront pas!" spirit. The really lively sentries were either Senegalese or Indo-Chinese. They were distinctly hostile to my unfamiliar uniform. Even some of the officers seemed resigned to defeat. One major at Rheims with a title going back many hundreds of years said, when we were buying champagne, "You may as well drink it up; the Germans will soon have the lot!" I cannot say I was exactly standing on the ramparts myself peering towards the enemy horde with my sword in my hand. I was young and very happy to be in France. I thoroughly enjoyed the freedom from peace-time routines and restrictions. I missed the companionship of my wife and children but otherwise I spent those months, supremely content, sitting on the edge of a volcano.

Yet when the Germans invaded Belgium on 10th May, it came as a shattering surprise. Did no one remember 1914 when they came in exactly the same way? I suppose we had the impregnable Maginot Line at the back of our minds but of that I will speak later.

I had few contacts with our own army in France, as I was concerned almost wholly with air matters, but at least our troops were business-like enough. I remember, towards the end when the roads were chaotic with refugees and retreating soldiers, one Guardsman trying to bring some order into the panic and confusion. The Germans were not far behind but he stood there with his "Pass along quickly, sir, please!" as if he were a policeman in Piccadilly Circus. Everyone who got out of France safely at that time should thank the riflemen who held Calais to the end. Yet that gallant episode is not often remembered today.

III

From the house in the avenue de la Ferté-sous-Jouarre I planned my journeys and wrote my reports. For the first few days everything was quiet and I had time to settle down and get to know all kinds of people from the Commander-in-Chief downwards. My sole contact with the great man was not a happy one. He came on a tour of inspection one day. We were lined up, a dozen or so officers in each room. Our group captain accompanied him, introducing each officer with a few words about his job. Eventually I found myself face to face with the air marshal. He stood with his hands on his hips and with his feet apart. He looked me up and down, noted the absence of wings or medal ribbons above my left breast pocket and his eyes said, "Good God, is the Royal Air Force reduced to this?" The group captain explained that I had just come out to do the job of examining and reporting on shot-down enemy aircraft. "What do you look for?" asked the air marshal. I gave him the full answer forgetting nothing. This most certainly did not please him. "What about this new supercharger they've got?" he asked. I said quite truthfully that I had never heard of it. At this he threw up his hands in despair. The war was clearly lost and I had lost it. He went on, suggesting that some people might learn their jobs before they came out. Trying to help, I ventured to put forward the proposal that a couple of weeks of training at Farnborough might be useful but the air marshal did not think this was a good idea. Before abandoning me to an uncertain fate, he recommended that I should learn my job properly. "I shall do my best, sir!" I said in my bravest Boy Scout manner. "I'm sure you will!" he replied in an ominous tone and passed on to the next victim. This interview, at which I had hoped to shine with a bright light, depressed me very much until, half an hour after the air marshal's departure, the group captain sent down one of his officers with this message – "The group captain's compliments. Not to worry. The air marshal only heard about that supercharger himself last night in the mess."

After two days as a supernumerary in No. 2 Mess I was transferred as a founder member of the newly formed No. 5 Mess in the avenue de Rebais at the end of which stood the statue of the gallant Beaurepaire. No. 5 Mess was in a pleasant house in a large garden along the bottom of which flowed the Grand-Morin. The P.M.C. was a distinguished meteorologist with the rank of group captain and there were about fifteen members, mainly Met officers. I at last acquired a very comfortable feather bed in a little room under the roof.

Though it was a large house, there was only one bathroom in which an erratic geyser threatened to explode at any moment. To shave without haste I was in the habit of getting up half an hour earlier than the others. This gave me a free half-hour in the garden before breakfast at eight. The spring had come like a green mist in the trees and the garden was full of primroses, primulas and violets.

In the evening our usual rendezvous was the "Ours", a bar and restaurant reserved for British and French officers. Why it was called "The Bear" I never discovered. The proprietor was Marius, a fat jovial character with as choice a flow of bad language as I have ever heard. He was a veritable Larousse of pornographic expressions. During the day he was a member of a French Army signals unit but, after duty, he laid aside his uniform and became the "Patron de l'Ours". Every evening he presided at the bar and roared obscenities to those of us who could understand.

If we stayed in the mess, we usually had a concert of old music-hall songs to the accompaniment of a piano. No. 5 Mess could be heard streets away. We occasionally had French officers as guests and they sang their songs, not always translatable into polite English. This encouraged similar efforts from the R.A.F. In those days the R.A.F. had a repertoire of bawdy ballads, many of which were sung to hymn tunes. By one of the happiest accidents of the war, we had a French corporal attached to our mess as *chef de cuisine*. How we came to acquire this treasure I do not know but, as an ex-chef from Boulestin, he was indeed a treasure and we fed like princes. I once mentioned that I had never eaten tripe. He suggested *tripe à la mode de Caen* for · dinner one evening. It was superb. However, this high living was the cause of our undoing. We were warned one day that the Air Vice-Marshal would be coming to lunch on a tour of inspection of messes. An air vice-marshal does not come to lunch every day and we decided to pull out all the stops and give him the lunch of his life.

For days our corporal chef worked in the kitchen planning a lunch which would have made a Lord Mayor's banquet look like corned beef hash. The day of the lunch arrived and we very respectfully led our guest into the ante-room. The French windows were open and he chose to sit on the railing outside to have his apéritif which had to be non-alcoholic. The railing began to give way under him and we hauled him back into the room only just in time.

The table looked magnificent. We had borrowed all over the town to make a good show. The first course came on and then our Air Vice-Marshal announced that he was a dyspeptic and was limited to soda water and the simplest of foods, preferably toast or dry biscuits. We had toast but that was for the caviar. So there he sat like Odysseus, glowering terribly, as this feast of Lucullus proceeded. It was nearly three o'clock before he was able to take his leave of us. We were all feeling very mellow. Even if the Air Vice-Marshal had not enjoyed it, we had. But our joy was not to last. On the morrow a circular was received reducing our messing allowance!

The happy days of junketings at the "Ours", concerts and our excellent French cuisine soon came to an end, at least for me. Real war still seemed remote until I was told that my first job in the field was to take me to the German frontier. I had a driver who carried a rifle and I was given a Colt 4.5 revolver, very similar to the one which my grandfather carried in the American Civil War.

My first stop was at Rheims, which was the H.Q. of our Advanced Air Striking Force, known as A.A.S.F. or Panther. I went by way of Château Thierry, birthplace of La Fontaine and a town full of memories of the 1914 war. H.Q. at Rheims was at the Château Polignac but unofficial H.Q. was at the "Lion d'Or". The latter I was to get to know much later. I received my orders at the Château, picked up another officer and we set off for a place north-east of Bitche, which I noticed to my horror was located between the Maginot and Siegfried Lines. Our route was through Suippes to Ste Menehould, where Louis XVI and his family were recognized on the flight to Varennes. On the road we passed Valmy and I thought of old Kellermann and Belloc's little essay. From Ste Menehould we went to Verdun, where I saw the great memorial for the first time, and thence to Metz. There was just light enough to have a glimpse of the cathedral before the black-out descended on us.

We put up at the Hôtel Royal and in the morning made contact with the last outpost of the R.A.F. at the Caserne Ney. From then onwards we were on our own as we left for St Avold and Sarreguemines through the Maginot Line. As we approached Sarreguemines we asked all sentries on the road through the line if the town was in the hands of the French or the Germans. We knew there had been some fighting there. No one knew or seemed to care very much. Suddenly we were stopped by a road barrier bearing the dramatic notice –

Route Barrée
Route en vue à l'ennemi!

Well, here was the war at last! No sound disturbed the peace of the countryside, no shot or shell, no martial clamour, no rat-tat-tat of machine guns. We decided that this was no occasion to seek the bubble reputation in the cannon's mouth. The barrier was impassable in any case so we planned to by-pass Sarreguemines to the south. No one knew the way anywhere. We finally found our way to Sarralbe and then to Sarre-Union. But we were going south and Bitche was to the east. The Sarre had to be crossed somewhere and we eventually got over at Herbitzheim. The river was in flood and the bridge appeared to have sunk. There was no one in sight to give us any information – I expected at least a guard on the bridge – so we opened the doors of the car in case the bridge collapsed, which it looked like doing at any moment, and over we went at water level. It was still no man's land on the other side as we drove on in the direction of Bitche.

We were now beyond the Maginot Line and making straight for Germany and the Siegfried Line. The absence of any life at all made us imagine ambushes round every corner and our enthusiasm decreased as we progressed. At last we came to Bitche, an uninteresting little garrison town, and reported to French Army and Air H.Q. at the barracks. The French Air Force strength there consisted of half a dozen officers under a commandant, who was a most engaging personality. In this dreary spot I suppose it was a relief to see even us. He made us welcome, gave us food in the mess and prepared to accompany us to a point close to the frontier where a German aircraft had been shot down. Our little procession of cars started off. Near our destination we came within sight of the enemy, according to the commandant. We had to drive up a road on a kind of ridge which, the commandant informed me, was fired on if a procession of cars went up but was unmolested if the cars went up one at a time. Thus we went up severally while I reassured myself with the thought that the Germans are a very methodical people. Happily they proved to be so and we all arrived at the site of the crash without mishap.

The wreckage was of no great interest beyond the identification of the unit. The French gave me a copy of their report and that was good enough for me, as at that moment an artillery bombardment started up. Up till then my only experience of artillery had been guns in Hyde Park on the King's birthday. Then I heard a queer whistling overhead followed by dull explosions mercifully a long way off. I asked as nonchalantly as possible what it was all about and was told that the French had started firing and that the Germans were replying. The whistling sound was the shells overhead! This apparently happened every day. Then I began to think that, if one *must* be mixed up in artillery fire, the best place to be would be in the middle of the trajectory. Fortunately it did not occur to me until later that the range, on one side at least, could be shortened.

We got down the road to Bitche safely and left soon afterwards for Metz. That was no easy task. To begin with, we had the flooded Sarre to negotiate, this time in the darkness. From Bitche to Herbitzheim is no great distance but we lost our way again and again. We must have been almost there when we were challenged by a black French soldier. With the greatest difficulty we persuaded him that we were not Germans, after which he tried to be helpful. In fact, in his anxiety to assist, he sent us back in the opposite direction. I estimated that we must have been well on the way to Germany by the time we turned again. Anyway we crossed the Sarre three times that night before we got on to the road to St Avold again.

It was one thing to get through the Maginot Line from the right side but to come back from the direction of the German frontier was another matter. To begin with, we made our return journey in the dark. Without headlamps this was uncomfortable enough but every few hundred yards a lantern was waved across the road. We had to stop and establish our identity before being allowed to go on. Mostly the sentries were French colonial soldiers, who had a habit of holding their bayonets at the ready within an inch or two of my intestines and keeping a finger on the trigger of their rifles. As their knowledge of French was very slight and as the colour of an R.A.F. uniform did not differ very much from that of the Wehrmacht uniform, we had the greatest difficulty in justifying our presence there. I was marched back to dozens of Postes and guardrooms to explain to a sleepy officer who

I was. I was told later by another R.A.F. officer that he surmounted such difficulties by producing an insurance policy with a large red seal on it. This greatly impressed France's overseas soldiers and he was usually allowed to proceed at once.

We had to get back to Metz with the minimum of delay to telephone our report to Panther and all these halts were maddening. Then, to crown it all, we ran out of petrol. We were about a mile beyond the last hold-up which was in a village. I had to tramp back in the dark expecting to be shot at any minute. I managed to find a guardroom in which a number of French soldiers were asleep on piles of hay, each separated from his neighbour by an upright board. They took me to a captain who was still up, drinking in a little estaminet. The captain was commandant of the village. Everyone was in bed, he said, but if I wanted petrol I should have it. While we were being filled up, he told me his life history. A veteran of the 1914 war, he was still awaiting promotion after eighteen years. Here again I had the impression that no one cared a damn if the Germans arrived that night. I doubt if that crowd of tired and bored men lying on the hay could have done much about it.

IV

We put through our call at the Caserne Ney, had a quick look at Metz and set off for Rheims. On the way back we had more leisure to see the country. The main Maginot Line is shown on the maps as passing through a point about halfway between Metz and Sarreguemines, but in depth the defences extended considerably on each side. It took quite a long time to pass through the whole defence system.

Right across the country over the hills ran the lines of tank traps like the Great Wall of China. Machine-gun nests at strategic points on the road, little slits in hillsides betraying an underground post, a curl of smoke coming up from the middle of a field together with miles of barbed wire contributed to what would have been a formidable barrier for ground troops. The main defence works were of course underground and I gather that what one saw was only the tip of the iceberg. My "War Map of the Western Front" dated October 1939 shows the Maginot Line extending from Basle in Switzerland to a point near Furnes on the Belgian coast. As far as I could find out in my wanderings, it stopped at Sedan.

As we passed through Verdun to Rheims the ravages of the 1914 war were still apparent. It was saddening to think that, instead of reconstructing this shattered country, we were once again at the beginning of another war of destruction. The people who had come back to their ruined towns and villages after 1918 had had to leave them again. Here and there were the cemeteries; British, French, German and Italian. In almost every village was the standard iron and concrete memorial with the Gallic cock triumphant –

AUX ENFANTS
DE
SAINT-JEAN-LES-DEUX-JUMEAUX
MORTS POUR LA FRANCE
1914–1918

Yet here we were again with another generation of the children of Saint-Jean-les-Deux-Jumeaux marching off to war as they did to Verdun and the Chemin des Dames.

We had some curious encounters on this road through the line. One night my car almost collided with a French car going in the opposite direction. We both pulled up and three French Air Force officers rolled out of the other car. They were clearly on the way back to their post after a riotous party. I complained in the midst of much handshaking and Entente Cordiale that we were continually held up by sentries for questioning. Without any hesitation they gave me the password. All I had to do was to shout out "Le mot est Duroc!" and all would be well. After that, we went through without any trouble. The sentries cried out "Passez! Passez!" and retired with their red lamps. Nevertheless I felt some misgiving that a password to get through France's main defence could be given so freely.

East of Metz this trip through the line was always depressing. Each evacuated village had been turned into a barracks and a slum. There were no women or children. An enormous amount of horse-drawn transport had churned up the roads into mud-tracks. The soldiers seemed to have nothing to do. They never knew anything and it was hopeless to ask for directions. There were no signposts and my map references for shot-down aircraft were vague if not misleading.

After a short stay in Coulommiers again, I had to go to Nancy to examine a shot-down aircraft near Lunéville. In the meantime I had some formal liaison jobs with the French Air Force H.Q. under General Vuillemin at Montceaux, where I inspected the château which Henri IV had given to Gabrielle d'Estrées. My liaison was with the Deuxième Bureau and at times with the Cinquième Bureau, the technical intelligence branch. Here the French were most co-operative.

The road to Nancy led through Sézanne. Vitry-le-François, St Dizier and Toul. On my journeys eastwards I had several memorable meals at the Hôtel de France at Sézanne, renowned for the local trout and excellent wines. Before reaching Toul, we took a wrong turning and found ourselves in a village called Domrémy-la-Pucelle, my second contact with Joan of Arc. We had no time for sightseeing and pressed on to Nancy, where we had a small H.Q. known as Eagle East. H.Q., B.A.F.F. was known as Eagle.

The crash I had come to inspect was near Lunéville, to the south-east of Nancy. It was late when we arrived so I stayed the night at the Hôtel d'Angleterre. This was quite a honeymoon establishment, as

French officers were allowed to entertain their wives there even though they were on active service. Perhaps this *was* the active service!

Early next morning I left for Lunéville. On the road I noticed two tall towers of a church which quite dominated the landscape. It was the church of Saint-Nicolas-du-Port, one of the finest churches of Lorraine. With its towers nearly three hundred feet high it is said to rank with the cathedrals of Metz and Toul. I made a note to have a closer look after the inspection at Lunéville.

A day or two before my arrival there had been an air battle between a French Morane fighter and a Messerschmitt 110, which resulted in the Messerschmitt crashing into solid Lorraine clay from a height of about 20,000 feet. The remains were still being excavated when I arrived. When it was dug out it was found that the engines had penetrated to a depth of over fifteen feet. Examination of the wreckage, as it was recovered, was not easy. Every instrument and other pieces of mechanism were covered with clay or mud, which did not help identification. To make things harder, crowds surged round the pit we had to dig. Any piece of metal which escaped our notice was likely to be carried off as a souvenir. In fact we had to arrange with the police later to have some of the souvenir-hunters traced and the pieces brought back. Anything with an inscription or manufacturer's date on it was of value to us but unfortunately an inscription in German made it all the more interesting to the people in the town.

As far as the crew of two was concerned, little remained but scraps of flesh and shreds of uniforms. One grisly souvenir eventually appeared which caused great excitement – a gold signet ring with the initials HB on a severed finger. "Un doigt de Boche!" cried the crowd ecstatically. Everyone, including two demure-looking nuns, surged round to catch a glimpse of it. I am afraid that HB was the only clue we had to identify the poor airman. Later, the ammunition drums of the 20 mm cannon were recovered. We had to know the order in which the shells were fired, for instance, tracer, ball, explosive and so on. But the drums were packed with mud, shells and human remains. A man at the French Air Force Parc d'Aérostation at Rehainvillers was given the job of removing the rounds and laying them out in order of firing. It was not a pleasant job. He had a meat skewer and a tin of chloride of lime. Halfway through the job, the bell sounded for lunch. He dropped his skewer and I saw him rush straight off to the table where he sat down and got on with his meal. What with the smell and the horrors of the morning's excavation, I decided to restrict my own lunch to a strong drink.

Considering the almost complete destruction of the German aircraft, we managed to obtain quite a lot of useful information. The Germans *are* a very methodical people and they had manufacturers' plates with addresses and serial numbers on much of their equipment, which in the long run gave us quite a good idea of who made what.

But that was not the end of the story of the crash at Lunéville. Though the Morane fighter had its tail almost shot away and though the pilot was severely wounded, he managed to make a belly landing. A crowd of people rushed to the aircraft and, in assisting him from the cockpit, someone inadvertently pressed the machine-gun button. The machine-guns went off, killing eight people and wounding many others. The only consolation was that the cannon, which fired through the airscrew boss, did not go off as well. I saw the Morane later at Rehainvillers and they told me that the cannon was still loaded at the time with plenty of rounds to spare.

On the way back I did inspect the church of Saint-Nicolas-du-Port. It was a fine piece of architecture in the Gothic style of Lorraine dating from the fifteenth and sixteenth centuries. The two great towers were most impressive and there was a fine Entombment of Christ in a crypt beneath the altar. I am afraid that, whether they liked it or not, my drivers had quite an education in ecclesiastical architecture. They usually appeared interested and on one occasion I found one of them kneeling in prayer in the cathedral at Châlons.

I had to hasten back to Coulommiers, as La Tosca had invited us all to a show in her cinema. La Tosca was a rather flamboyant blonde of about thirty-five who occasionally visited the "Ours". She sang for us once there. Hence the name "La Tosca". Her husband, a poor little weed of a man, was known as "Le Moustique", according to Marius. Any other remarks of Marius on this rather Clochemerle *ménage* are not fit for publication.

Life in Coulommiers was highly respectable save for the existence of "Numéro Trois". No. 3 rue de l'Aré was the very shabby brothel of the town. We used to pass it on the way to H.Q. and exchange greetings with the rather unglamorous inmates at the windows. No women appeared at the "Ours" with the exception of La Tosca and the wife of Marius. Madame sometimes brought her baby to be admired, while Marius stood by glowing with pride under a show of complete indifference.

Before I left on my next assignment, which was Sedan, I solved the mystery of the Santees. Much of the work at our Intelligence H.Q. appeared to be concerned with the production of the Santees. One overheard people saying, "That will do for the Santees. See that it goes in." Towards the end of the day, one of the flight lieutenants from upstairs would cry out, "Any more for the Santees?" Being still a newcomer I did not dare to ask what the Santees was or were. There are all kinds of shibboleths for new boys in any service and one picks up the jargon as one goes along. I did not want to display my ignorance. Moreover I could not imagine that any effort of mine could contribute to such an important institution as the Santees. I should mention at this point that, though we had a few officers who were good French scholars, the general level in our H.Q. was low. Eventually some intelligence I had brought in was deemed worthy of inclusion in the mysterious Santees and I at last discovered that this was the *synthèse* or synthesis of the day's intelligence from all sources, destined for the C.-in-C. Any attempt to pronounce it in the French way would have sounded pretentious and Santees it remained.

V

We heard from the H.Q. of the French 2nd Army near Vouziers that a German aircraft had been shot down in an almost inaccessible part of the woods east of Sedan and I was invited to go and inspect it. I looked at the map and found I was bound for the frontier again. Fortunately it was the Luxembourg frontier this time. Another officer had by now joined me to learn the trade. He spoke French and German and also had the advantage of having spent some time with the Luftwaffe on a peace-time course.

We had passed Rheims and had reached Pont-Faverger on the road to Vouziers when our car went up in flames. Petrol tanks were often filled from cans or drums when no proper filling pump was available. At our last fill-up petrol must have spilled over the end of the car and on the rear axle. I can only imagine that a spark struck from the road must have set us on fire. Anyhow we smelt something burning, pulled up and the three of us just got out in time, each with his bag, before the whole car was on fire. It was a wonderful spectacle for the whole village. A fire extinguisher was produced and the flames were overcome before the tank could explode. One hero had his eyebrows and the front of his hair burnt off but he seemed to welcome the opportunity of exhibiting his skill with the extinguisher. The car now looked like a forlorn wedding cake. We left it where it stood – there were no traffic wardens in those days – and went to the military post in the centre of Pont-Faverger. We had a car sent out from Rheims to rescue us but it arrived too late for us to continue our journey that day. We spent the night at the "Lion d'Or" in Rheims and made a fresh start the next day.

We had to turn right before reaching Vouziers for the village of Cernay. Here, amid a chaos of small muddy streets, we found the château which was the headquarters of General Roques. Over one door was a carved stone inscription in Gothic characters stating that His Imperial and Royal Highness the Crown Prince of Germany had his headquarters there during the 1914 war. Little Willie was certainly a bonus for the French at that time.

We were received by Colonel Péquin, the General's Chief of Staff, a grey-haired French Air Force officer with four rows of medal ribbons. After a session with his Deuxième Bureau we were invited to the mess for lunch. The meal proceeded in a dignified manner, my friend and I doing our Entente Cordiale act. Then suddenly in the midst of the meal, the colonel stood up, raised his glass and led the whole mess in their *chanson de popote* or mess song. This was a ribald chant of which I could only catch the last line of each verse. This was –

Et merde à ces cochons d'Hitler!

so the rest may well be imagined.

After lunch the colonel presented me with a pass and a copy of an etching he had made of the entrance hall of the château. Then, accompanied by an officer of the Deuxième Bureau, we continued our journey to Sedan by way of Vouziers.

Sedan was a colourless, uninteresting and largely deserted town. Remembering the events of 1870 I cannot say that I felt very happy at the thought of the German armies little more than an hour's drive from where we were. I had been reading Octave Aubry's *Napoléon III*. Later I walked up the road where he sat in his carriage, broken in health and spirit, to hand over France to the enemy. I little realized that we were within a few weeks of a much more shameful Sedan.

We now had to find a place called Pouru-aux-Bois, east of Sedan on the border of France and Luxembourg. About a week earlier, a Dornier 17 had flown over the French fortifications near Sedan on a photographic reconnaissance. Later I saw the photographs at Cernay. On the way back the Dornier had been intercepted by a Morane and had been shot down. For four days the wreck had remained with its crew of three undiscovered in the dense marshy woods close to Pouru-aux-Bois. It had eventually been found accidentally by some men on manoeuvres in the woods.

One member of the crew had been caught in the wreckage, suspended by the neck and had died there. One must have died just before the discovery, after lingering without food and drink for four days. He was still warm when found. The third was unconscious but still alive, pinned under part of the wreckage and some trees which had been knocked down in the crash. The survivor must have been tough, as he had already recovered to some extent and had been interrogated in the hospital.

That was the story. The aircraft was still in the woods and we had to get to it. After much discussion with the French it was decided that the only vehicle which could negotiate this wooded swamp was a *tout-terrain*. This curious contraption eventually appeared. I have since seen projects for vehicles to traverse the surface of the moon. In many ways they resembled a *tout-terrain*. It was a cross between a tank-like lorry, an armoured car and a tractor. It had eight wheels in unexpected places. The hubs of the wheels appeared to be attached to tubes which went up and down so that at a given moment, when negotiating a sudden bump in the ground, some of the wheels could be higher than others. We sat on the floor of the vehicle and held on to anything we could reach. The crew came aboard, swore, kicked things and pulled levers. With a frightful explosion we leapt forward at a good 4 m.p.h. It was moderately uncomfortable until we entered the woods. After that, rounding the Corbière lighthouse on a rough day was a pleasure trip. A ship is at least governed by certain laws of physics. This thing defied even the laws of gravity. It pitched, it rolled, it poised at angles from which it could never recover – and then recovered. It sank in mud two feet deep, it rode over incredible mounds, it smashed small trees, it hung on perilous ledges and confidently crashed on. Then we reached a patch near the wreckage which defied even a *tout-terrain*. Though this promised even more discomfort, I was glad to know that there was something a *tout-terrain* could not do and which human beings could. So we alighted into mud which squelched at the top of our gum boots. Only by clinging to branches were we able to draw our feet along with horrible sucking sounds. I could well imagine the state of mind of those two men, stuck in that desolation for four days and unable to move.

The aircraft had landed on reasonably firm ground and in its fall it had made quite a clearing in which we could work. One engine was thrown in one direction and the other some way from it. The rest of what had been a graceful, streamlined aircraft was now a confused heap of metal. We made our examination and wrote up the notes for our report while the French guard searched for pieces of aluminium tubing for making up into napkin rings for the mess. We then began our Tarzan-like progress back to the *tout-terrain*, which monstrous vehicle duly delivered us back to Pouru-aux-Bois. Still, we had to be grateful. There would have been no other way of getting to that Dornier 17.

The cause of the crash was a hit in one engine. The prisoner said that they had been attacked by eight Moranes. The Dornier's task was to photograph the French second positions. It had completed its mission when it was intercepted on the way back. Apart from the photographs, which were excellent, we managed to get enough information for a fairly full report on the unit and where it was based, on armament, fuel, radio, de-icing and so on, despite the extensive damage. From the engines, nine-cylinder radials with three-bladed airscrews, our experts would be able to work out the performance.

As far as I could find out, the fortifications which the crew of that Dornier 17 had so ably photographed formed the end of the Maginot Line, despite the reassuring "War Map of the Western Front" and the red line along the French-Belgian frontier. There seemed to be little in the way of defences – to my admittedly un-military mind at least – to the left of Sedan. I had occasion to slip across the frontier into Belgium before 10th May to examine aircraft shot down there. The only barrier I encountered was the usual red and white frontier pole, which was politely lifted to let me in. I did see some barbed wire at Sedan but we were able to step over it.

The next few weeks were taken up with several crashes of no great interest, with visits to Rheims to drink champagne at the "Lion d'Or" and liaison with the French equivalent of Farnborough, which was at Orléans-Bricy. Here we exchanged information on German aircraft and I tried to find some excuse to do a tour of the châteaux of the Loire. It did not work. When I finally did leave Orléans after Dunkirk I was in far too much of a hurry to do any sightseeing.

Orléans was my third encounter with the shade of Joan of Arc. Here I was served with the corny old joke which is one of the local traditions. "Do you know that Joan of Arc produced quite a large family?" "But," you reply, "she was the *Maid* of Orleans – la Pucelle!" Then comes the punch line – "Go to the Square of the Martyrdom and you will see 'les dix fils' [l'édifice] of Joan of Arc."

I also managed to get one trip to Paris. Permits for Paris were hard to get. The English to this day are inclined to look upon Paris as the City of Sin and so it was put out of bounds without a permit. One officer did run off to Paris to see a girl and was absent for some days. To save him from being posted as a deserter, two of us slipped up to Paris to persuade him to return. With great difficulty we got him home and sobered him up by the next morning. My own legal trip was to act as an interpreter for our Persian-speaking wing commander who wanted to buy a wireless set.

So we went on in our little Goshen, unmindful of the volcano under our feet. Reynaud had formed his new government, the Germans had invaded Denmark and Norway and we had landed troops near Narvik. Incredibly the Belgians did not stop army leave till 11th April. On 27th April Ribbentrop justified the invasion of Norway in a German White Book. In 1945 I found a copy of his speech on the subject in the ruins of the Italian Embassy in Berlin. We also heard that British troops had relieved a French division on the Sarre front.

Early in May I was in Orléans again with my young colleague. We were working with a squadron leader from H.Q., a veteran of the 1914 war, who entertained us one evening in a rather doubtful establishment with a copious supply of food and drink.

The following morning, both of us were on our way to a café in search of black coffee. There on the terrace sat our squadron leader in the morning sunlight, sober as a judge. He invited us to join him for coffee. We had scarcely had time to drink it before a British Army despatch rider roared up on his motorcycle and, ascertaining our names, announced that the Germans had invaded Holland, Belgium and Luxembourg. It was 10th May.

VI

With instructions to join Air Component H.Q. at Maroeuil near Arras, we were on our way within half an hour. We arrived that night by way of Coulommiers and Chauny, which was known as Eagle North and later became H.Q. after Arras was overrun. Maroeuil was a short way up the St Pol road out of Arras. It looked none too inviting as a residence so I decided to put up at the Hôtel de l'Univers at Arras. One of the advantages of having an unusual job is that no one knows where to fit you in. The Admin. people are therefore glad to get rid of you as soon as they can and leave you to your own resources. This left me free to choose a more comfortable billet though, as events turned out, the Hôtel de l'Univers was not such a happy choice.

While we were driving up to Arras, a large fleet of Junkers 52s were towing gliders into the Belgian fortress of Eben Emael, the capture of which was one of the first shocks delivered by the Germans. Increased air activity in general had resulted in quite a number of shot-down aircraft in northern France. With only two officers engaged on picking up the pieces, we split up and henceforth I was on my own again.

I was back in the First World War. I was eight years old in 1914 and many of the towns and villages through which I passed in 1940 were headline news in those days. I had heard my uncle, who was killed on the first day of the Battle of the Somme in 1916, speak of Albert, Béthune, La Bassée, Cambrai and many others, which would never have been heard of, had they not been the meeting places of great armies. Who would have heard of Waterloo or Austerlitz if Napoleon had not passed that way? Since 1919 all these places in the valleys of the Somme and the Ancre had been rebuilt, the Virgin and Child on the top of the spire of the church at Albert, where they had hung suspended horizontally throughout the first war, had been re-gilded and set up again and the fields had been ploughed and sown where the war had left nothing but rubble and death. Yet here we were again, in country where one can scarcely take a few steps without walking over a British soldier's grave. In all the area up to Brussels, which I had to cover, the soldiers of Marlborough, Wellington and Haig had marched and fought and chased the village girls and died. Then the peasants came back and life went on.

One of the first shot-down aircraft reported to me was at Agne near Arras. With no signposts and only a very vague map reference, I had some difficulty in locating this crash. Eventually, having almost given up the chase, I found two peasants working in a field, an old man and his wife. I asked them if they had heard of an "avion boche abbatu". They shook their heads and got on with their work. I thought then that I would walk to the top of a rise at the end of the field, which might give me a view of the surrounding country. There in the adjoining field was my Heinkel bomber on its belly, almost intact. It had crashed with its undercarriage retracted, both wings and tail having been well shot up. One engine had overheated owing to damage to the cooler. The crew, dead or alive, had been removed and no guard left. It was rather a find for us, as two additional machine guns had been mounted one on each side of the fuselage, firing to the side and aft. The aircraft had come down within a few hundred yards of the field where the two old people were working. I told them about it on my way back to the car but they still went on working.

I had another Heinkel bomber to investigate at Marquillies near La Bassée. This was a complete wreck. I can only think that the bombs had exploded on impact. It was said that three of the crew had been captured, so they must have baled out. One body lay among the wreckage. The head was missing. This was my first dead body and it was a very unpleasant shock to see this young man lying there while groups of people from the village strolled over to have a look at the dead *boche*. I assured myself that the French must have gone through his pockets, so I covered him up with a sheet of metal from the crash. All I got out of that wreck were a few manufacturers' name plates.

A little later I had a further unpleasant experience in a village near the frontier. A farm worker told me that an aircraft had crashed close by. When I got there I found it was a Hurricane, the first of our own which I had seen. Apart from reporting it, there was nothing more to do and I was about to leave when I was horrified to see a scalp on the top of the fuselage. I had heard that the pilot had been buried near by and apparently his scalp, no doubt torn off as he crashed, had been

A formation of Heinkel IIIs . . .

. . . and how some of them landed up. Heinkel and other German
bombers in a junk yard somewhere in England.

Dornier 17 bombers over the East End of London in 1940. German Battle of Britain picture.

And one which did not get back. A shot-down Dornier 17 under guard in an English field.

found afterwards. The curly hair with the parting still intact lay there in the morning sunshine where I left it.

The first three days after my arrival in Arras furnished more German aircraft than I could handle. There were crashes at Lillers, Béthune, Valenciennes, St Amand, Roubaix, Lille, Douai, La Bassée and in little villages which I can no longer find on the map. Most of them were Heinkel 111 bombers. There was one Junkers 88, one of the outstanding aircraft produced by the Germans in the last war. One Heinkel at Herlies had been shot down by a Spitfire. One member of the crew had saved himself by parachute and the rest had been killed. In the general disorder after 10th May it was only rarely that credit could be given for a crash as we could later in the Battle of Britain. It could be anyone's anti-aircraft fire or British, French or Belgian fighters. It was also difficult to trace crews for interrogation. They had usually been picked up by the time I arrived, though now and again I found a survivor in the local police station.

There was no time for detailed reports. A pro forma report lettered from A to O provided the essential facts without trimmings. I used to think of it as the Alpha and Omega report, according to the Book of Revelation, in which it says, "I am Alpha and Omega, the first and the last".

We drove all day from one wreck to another, filling up the pro forma for each and rushing back at night to Maroeuil to get our signals off. By this time my drivers were able to help. They came to know what to look for and sometimes made useful discoveries, especially when a wreck was spread over a few hundred yards of ground.

On the night of the 14th I got back to Maroeuil fairly early in the evening. I sent off my reports and promised myself that I would be in bed at the Hôtel de l'Univers in Arras at 9.30 writing a letter to my wife. I knew she would be worried after the events of 10th May. As we drove through the darkness towards Arras we could see a glow in the sky. Someone on the road told us that the Germans had been dropping incendiaries on the town. Nevertheless I was still determined to get an early night in spite of the anti-aircraft gun which was in the courtyard below my window on the third floor. Then suddenly we had to pull up as there had been an accident on the road. Two army vehicles had collided and a man was lying injured on the side of the road. I realized that my hopes of a good night's sleep were fading rapidly. We could have got by but we could not leave the man there.

So we got out and made him comfortable. He asked for a cigarette and I sat there with him while I sent my driver back to Maroeuil for an ambulance. We duly packed him off and drove on to Arras arriving between 11 and midnight. So much for my early night and my wife's letter. As we drew near to the Hôtel de l'Univers, I realized that it was no longer there. After the preliminary incendiary raid, the Germans had bombed Arras. Where my third-floor bedroom had been was now empty sky under a bright moon. We later heard that they dug out about thirty bodies. At first I did not take it in. Then, when I thought that I would have been in bed at 9.30 had it not been for the injured man on the St Pol road, the reaction caused me to be violently sick. After that I felt better. It pays to be a Good Samaritan. My driver and I then spent an hour or two looking for incendiary bombs or anything else which the Germans might have dropped, after which I returned to Maroeuil and slept on the floor in one of the offices.

British and French troops had of course entered Belgium on 10th May and our No. 1 Corps and No. 2 Corps had set up their headquarters in Brussels. Mr Churchill had just told the House of Commons, "I have nothing to offer but blood and toil and tears and sweat." It was therefore with no great joy that I received orders to follow the British Army to Brussels.

We drove off on the morning of 15th May through Tournai, Leuze, Ath and Enghien. There were crashes to be inspected on the way up, a Heinkel 111 at Ormeignies near Ath and another at Huyssinghem near Hal. However, I was to have an extraordinary adventure at Enghien before we got to Hal.

As we progressed up the road to Brussels, we began to run into the first stream of refugees. There was quite a lot of military traffic going up to Brussels and we were in convoy most of the way. In the opposite direction there were cars full of fleeing civilians, farm carts, police and gendarmerie on bicycles all making for the French frontier. At Enghien, with British and Belgian troops passing through, the town was in a tumult. I decided to stay the night. My driver and I slept in the car, though air activity did not allow us much rest. In the morning we began a search for breakfast. A very frightened woman in a large house, close to which we had parked our car, let us shave in her kitchen and gave us bread and coffee. I noticed that, before she cut the new bread, she made the sign of the Cross on the bottom of the loaf. It was a simple gesture which stood out in my memory as much as the strange adventure which followed.

Shortly after we left her, in a profusion of her blessings and our thanks, we fell in with a colonel of the R.A.M.C., who considerably augmented our simple breakfast with tea and bacon. It was while I was sitting with him that the story began. A messenger brought a note to the table to say that a parachutist had been caught, dressed in Belgian uniform, on a roof in the town. As the only R.A.F. officer there, the matter was referred to me for judgement. What did I want to do with him? Was he to be shot? I should mention at this stage that civil administration was beginning to break down and no one, apart from the military authorities, was prepared to take any responsibility for anything. This was to get worse as the days went by and towns were almost completely abandoned in the general scramble southwards.

I said it was no business of mine, but it was pointed out that the Argylls were just leaving and the Belgian Army units were on the move. I was the only air expert and what were they to do? "Hand him over to the police!" I suggested. That wouldn't do, as the police had left the town! So here was I being asked to pronounce a death sentence over my breakfast.

The R.A.M.C. colonel and I had a lengthy discussion on military law, of which I knew practically nothing. The colonel, being a doctor, could have no part in sentencing a man to death. However, we reluctantly agreed that, if the man was a German parachutist in Belgian uniform, he should be shot. But who was going to do the shooting? A further message from the Belgian colonel, in whose charge the parachutist was, urged a quick decision. Why they thought that only an Air Force officer could deal with parachutists I simply could not understand.

Now I had never sentenced anyone to death before and it is not a job I would relish at the best of times. Finally I said they had better hand him over to the Argylls, wherever they were, and have him shot in the proper manner. After the messenger had left, I began to feel very uneasy and, though I had to press on to Brussels, I decided to go down and interrogate the prisoner before execution. So I drove down to the police station where the Belgian soldiers were guarding him. He was in a small one-ton covered truck in a yard at the side of the building. The Belgians opened the doors at the back of the truck and there, lying on the floor of the vehicle, was a man, tied hand and foot, nearly naked and groaning miserably. He looked more like a wild beast. He was covered with blood, his face was bruised and he was altogether a pitiful spectacle.

I told him, in German, that there was a good chance of his being shot and asked him if he had anything to say in his defence. No answer. I then spoke to him in French. At this he managed to turn over and said in French that he would like to explain himself to me. But first I had to get the guard to clear out half the population of Enghien, who also wanted to interrogate the prisoner, into the street. That made me very unpopular.

The man told me he was a Belgian. I tried to catch him out with an occasional question in German but he just did not understand. He had been mobilized at Mons, he said. He was not a parachutist at all!

I went back to the Belgians in the guard room and asked for the parachute and the man's uniform. They showed me the uniform but there was no parachute. It was suggested that he had pushed it down a chimney before he was caught. Now it is not an easy matter to push a parachute down a chimney on an ordinary house. I had the chimneys on the house searched but no trace of a parachute could be found. Then, quite by chance, a Belgian sergeant happened to say that he was from Mons, so I went out and asked the prisoner to name the C.O. at Mons when he joined up and to mention the name of any café opposite the railway station there. The answers were both correct. This man was no more a parachutist than I was.

Then I got the whole story. He was a deserter from the Belgian Army turned burglar in the absence of the police. He had been caught in uniform on the roof of this house and it had been concluded that he must have landed on the roof by parachute. He had a bullet wound in the upper part of his leg and it looked as if he had put up a fight before he was captured. I also had the impression that he had been rather roughly handled during the night in the Belgian guard room.

I put it to the Belgians that, as he was one of their own deserters, it was now a matter for the Belgian Army to have him court-martialled. Anyhow, I washed my hands of the whole affair since he was clearly no parachutist.

The Belgian colonel was reluctant to take him off my hands, but we eventually agreed that the least we could do would be to send him up to the hospital. So with a clear conscience I set off for Brussels. A day or two later I passed through Enghien again in the general retreat, so whatever else fate had in store for him, I do not think that military justice ever caught up with that cat-burglar.

VII

The stream of refugees increased as we approached Brussels. I had to break off to inspect the Heinkel bomber near Hal. It was burnt out and of little interest so I got back on the Brussels road as soon as I could. We were welcomed as heroes wherever we stopped. I felt far from heroic. It was 16th May and the Germans had deepened their thrust into Belgium. In fact I began to wonder if they would get to Brussels before I did. I doubted if my presence could have turned the tide of battle and felt inclined to join the refugees in the south-bound stampede. However, the Casabianca in me triumphed and I arrived in Brussels for the longest day's work I have ever done.

I duly reported to No. 1 Corps H.Q. and then to No. 2 H.Q., where I obtained information of shot-down aircraft. One of them was a Junkers 87 dive-bomber, which would have been our first specimen of this species. It was at Nosseghem on the road to Louvain. I made a note to examine it later after I had seen one crash at Vilvoorde on the outskirts of Brussels. In the meantime I was given an opportunity of interrogating the crew of the Ju 87. They were a choice pair of young thugs, very truculent, quite sure their side was winning and determined to give no information whatever. They stood stiffly to attention, each guarded by one of our soldiers with fixed bayonets at the ready. Having exhausted my routine questions, I asked them how they could bring themselves to bomb and machine-gun helpless women and children on the crowded roads. One could admire the prowess of the dive-bomber in battle but were they trained for this? The reply, from one of them, was very short, "Befehl ist Befehl!" (Orders are orders!) and that was that. There was no time to waste in philosophical discussion so I had them taken away.

That day I collected a whole list of aircraft to examine. There were crashes at Mutsaert, at Steen-Ockerzeel, at Stockel, at Iddergem and several other places, but no one had any map references. I interrogated four prisoners at No. 1 Corps H.Q. and planned to set out on a tour of the various crashes on the morrow. Evening was coming on but I felt I ought perhaps to make a start so I set off towards Malines to see if I could do at least one examination before nightfall. By the time I arrived anywhere near the alleged position of the aircraft, I realized I could not achieve much in the pitch dark and that there was quite a lot of noise over towards Malines. I did not know until later how near I was to the real war. Neither my driver nor I had had much sleep for some days, so I told him to turn round and drive me to the Metropole Hotel in Brussels where we could find a comfortable bed for a change.

It was very late when I marched into the Metropole and asked for two rooms. The man at the reception desk looked up alarmed. He examined my uniform to make sure I *was* British. Then he said, "Sir, do you know that the Germans are in the town?" It dawned on me in the matter of a fraction of a second that, as an intelligence officer, I had not been very bright. When I was at No. 1 Corps H.Q. earlier in the day, I had commented on the fact that they were burning papers. The same thing had happened at No. 2 Corps H.Q. I should have known that there is usually only one good reason why one burns one's papers. I should also have noticed that Brussels was strangely deserted as we drove in. The driver was standing at the door of the hotel. "Can you run?" I asked him. "Yes, sir, why?" he answered. "Then run for your bloody life!" I said and off we went to our car, which we had left round the corner. We had taken the distributor out for safety. While we were trying to put it in again, two figures with rifles and fixed bayonets loomed up out of the dark and said something, which I took to be German for a moment. This was the end. I saw myself as a prisoner of war for the next ten years in Upper Silesia. But it was not German, it was Flemish. They were two Belgian soldiers who had come in from somewhere near Malines. Would I take them to a Belgian unit?

Never were two guests more welcome. The three of us jammed into the back seats with their bayonets sticking out of the windows and we were off through the silent streets on the way to Lille as fast as the car could take us. Fortunately I knew the roads out of Brussels and we were soon clear of the suburbs. We passed through Hal and were approaching Enghien when I noticed a bright light in the sky above the town. I had heard in Brussels that Tournai, Leuze and Enghien had been bombed. Apparently part of Enghien was still burning. As we drove into the town I deposited my two friends. I had had little conversation with them in the car, as they spoke only Flemish. I gathered that they were Antwerp bargees who had been called up. They had been in some fighting to the east of Brussels and had somehow made their way into the town as far as the Metropole. There were Belgian soldiers in Enghien and they were glad to be among their own people again.

I made my way to the centre of the town where crowds of people were gathering to watch the fires. From Brussels to Enghien we had encountered almost no one on the road while Enghien was packed with townspeople, refugees and soldiers. As we pulled up, the car was surrounded by would-be passengers but I had to be quite firm or we would have had a dozen of them on top of the car as well as inside. I said I was on my way to Ath, Tournai and Lille. One man was very helpful. He pointed out my road but there were flames and smoke across it from fires on either side. No one incidentally was making any effort to put the fires out. It looked as if we were trapped till one man said that, if we made a dash for it, we could get through. The flames did not extend far down the street we had to take. I asked my driver if he was willing to try. He was only too anxious, so we closed the windows of the car while the crowd made room for us to start our run. I tried not to look as scared as I felt and off we went, hoping there would be no debris on the road. There was a horrible crunch of broken glass under the tyres as we went through the flames and smoke and then we were safe on the other side with a clear road before us. We checked to see that nothing was on fire on the outside of the car. We appeared to be intact, the tyres had survived the glass, so on we went to Lille, which we reached in the early morning.

I had lost my travelling kit in the bombing of the Hôtel de l'Univers at Arras. All I had now was a toothbrush, a cheap razor, a towel and a piece of soap I had bought before going up to Brussels. I found a hotel in the centre of the town and explained our plight to the proprietor. He showed us to two rooms which had wash basins. In five minutes we had washed and shaved and I was about to thank him for his courtesy when he announced he would have to charge us for the two rooms for the night. I said we had no intention of staying more than five minutes, but we had to pay. So this was the Entente Cordiale! Here I had come, at great personal discomfort, to fight on the side of La Belle France against our common enemy and here was this Frenchman doing me down with the Germans only a few miles off. However I comforted myself, as I paid up, with the thought that the Germans would shortly be taking over his whole hotel without worrying about paying the bill.

Our way now lay through Arras, Amiens and Beauvais to Paris. From now on the motive was to be *Festina lente*. The great exodus had really begun and the roads were to become a nightmare. Refugees set off with no destination in mind. All they wanted to do was get away. There were the patiently plodding peasants with their great farm carts, piled high with furniture and agricultural equipment and drawn by a stallion. Under the cart and attached to an axle was very often a tired dog. Then came the town folk in their family cars, packed with bedding, carpets and food. Lower down the social scale came those with prams and some with all their possessions on their backs. By the time we reached Amiens it was dark. The refugees rested by the roadside at night but we had to press on. It looked as if Amiens had been evacuated and this caused me to imagine Germans round every corner. I was glad to be clear of the town again and on the road to Beauvais.

Looking today at the situation map for 18th May 1940, I see that, between Brussels and Lille, I had passed through the area covered by the British Expeditionary Force. From Lille to Arras, the French First Army stood between me and the Germans, while the French Ninth Army covered my left flank as I journeyed from Arras to Amiens. But the Germans had already pushed through to Cambrai, south-east of Arras, while several arrows point past Péronne and St Quentin very close to Amiens. Had I known of this perilous situation at the time, I would have been scared out of my wits. At that time nobody seemed to know anything. The Germans might be round the corner or twenty miles away. It must be remembered that the fall of France happened within six weeks of the beginning of the German offensive, but events moved so quickly in the first week or ten days that the end was really decided then. I was often alone and out of touch with any military or air headquarters or units for days on end and could only guess where it was safe to venture. When we came in contact with a unit of any kind, we stocked up with food and, above all, petrol. The latter we carried in tin cans wired together and never let it out of sight. Refugees were not above siphoning petrol out of each other's cars at night in the mad rush to get somewhere south. Our reserve stock would have been a treasure. Many cars had to stop simply because they had run out of petrol. There were no pumps working. In fact there was nothing working. Shops were closed, police and fire stations had been abandoned together with all the administrative offices necessary for daily life. One could not be born or married, one could not even die properly, as there was no one to record such events.

My narrative may read as if I were battling alone amid turmoil, the only sane individual in a mad and disorderly world. Mine is a simple adventure story of one man doing a modest job on his own while a mighty struggle was going on all round on the ground and in the air. Our own air force was stretched to the utmost, risking even our home defence, a fact which was not realized by our ground forces who continually lamented the lack of air support. For a true account and appraisal of the great battle which was being fought then and which was to end at Dunkirk the reader must go to the British, French and German military historians. I was merely concerned with bringing back such information as I could gather and with keeping out of trouble.

After Beauvais we slept one night in the forest near Senlis. Here I had my one chance of changing history. I was looking at my maps and it struck me that we were quite close to Compiègne. It was in a clearing in the forest there that the Germans signed the armistice terms in Foch's railway coach in 1918. I knew the place. It was at Rethondes a little to the east of Compiègne itself. Since 1918 the coach had stood there together with a stone memorial commemorating the Allied victory and Germany's humiliation. Now it was practically certain that it would be overrun by the Germans in the next week or ten days. That would mean that the Germans would destroy it or, more likely still, make it the scene of France's humiliation if France fell.

At that time, 18th May, the situation of the French armies was not hopeless, despite the severe attacks which the Luftwaffe was carrying out on French rail and other communications. The Belgian Army had not yet capitulated. The trouble was that the French were fighting one kind of war and the Germans an entirely new war of opportunism, of movement and surprise, which only a few of the French like de Gaulle understood. The French high command was apparently at a loss to appreciate the enemy's intentions and, even if it did, to react quickly against a highly mobile force. Some time later, I had to go up from Rheims to a place called Neufchâtel on the Aisne, where I spent half a day in some French trenches. We had to stop on the road and drop down into communication trenches leading to what was then the

French front line. There stood the line of *poilus* with their steel helmets and their long bayonets fixed, just below the sandbags and barbed wire on top of the trench facing north. It could have been 1916.

From all I had seen and heard I did not feel very optimistic. I did not like the idea of that historic railway coach falling into Hitler's hands and, knowing the Germans, I had a premonition that they would take their revenge for the Versailles "Diktat", which had so often been the burden of Adolf Hitler's song, by humiliating the French there. In just over a month from that night I spent in the forest they did just that. I kept turning over in my mind the possibility of destroying the coach, either by burning it or getting a company of sappers to blow it up. I wish I had done so. It would have deprived Hitler of at least one of his triumphs. Then I thought – who am I to blow up a French national monument? To pin the Germans down in that railway coach in 1918 it had cost France nearly a million and a half dead, over two and a half million wounded and half a million prisoners or missing. In addition no small contribution had been made by our own people. Then I thought that the French would blow it up themselves and I was tired anyway, so I went to sleep. The following morning we drove to Chantilly and thence down to Paris.

VIII

The Germans had indeed reached Brussels on the night of my hasty departure. The British sensibly enough had left during the day. I thus had the distinction of being the last British officer to leave Brussels — through sheer stupidity. By the time I arrived in Paris, the German advance had been so rapid that they had practically overrun the route of my retreat southwards. They were progressing towards Ghent against the Belgian Army, westwards from Brussels against the B.E.F., which was falling back to hold the line of the Scheldt and the Lys, and were beginning to cut off the French First Army in a breakthrough past Cambrai in the direction of Arras. German arrows on the map were now pointing up in the first step to the encirclement of Dunkirk. Arras was soon cut off from the south. Lower down the French were still holding the line of the Somme and the Aisne, but the Germans were now in possession of the old Somme battlefield.

The British fought hard to hold Arras, which was almost surrounded, but the gallant attempt failed. Meanwhile the Germans to the south of Arras were pushing on past St Pol towards Boulogne, which they reached on 23rd May. The day after, they broke the British line on the Lys. Tournai, with its magnificent five-towered cathedral, birthplace of Clovis and Wolsey's bishopric before he became cardinal, was now in German hands. Further south Amiens was threatened and the Germans had captured Laon.

The Germans were only about sixty-five miles from Paris. Nothing much was or could be done about it. The French, according to General Gamelin, were unable to put any concentration of troops between Laon and Paris. Mr Churchill had seen the staff at the Quai d'Orsay burning their files a few days before. The French seemed resigned to the fall of Paris. It certainly would not have taken long for the German armour to get from Laon to Paris.

Yet it appeared, when I arrived in Paris, that the Parisians were in the midst of a sigh of relief. It was realized that the German tanks were not making for the capital. They had turned aside from that great prize, which even the Kaiser had not been able to win in the four years of the 1914 war. They were advancing instead to the Channel ports. Though it was clear that they were going to settle with the British and French round Dunkirk and to leave Paris over till later on, the danger was not imminent.

The British garrison was to withdraw from Arras on the evening of the 23rd. At the same time the Germans were pushing up the coast from Boulogne. Later they took Lille. In the meantime the Belgian Army capitulated and the stage was set for the Dunkirk evacuation.

On looking back, I can only wonder that there was not more of a panic. At my low level I did not know then of the recriminations going on among the French generals or the changes in the French government, which in any case did not make the least difference. The lack of fighting spirit I had noted in the Maginot Line seemed to be shared by the people at the top.

Paris was full of the wildest rumours but life went on much as before. However, I could not stay as I had much to report to Coulommiers. There I learned that H.Q. Advanced Air Striking Force was moving from Rheims to Troyes. Rheims was a little too close to the German armour. I was told that I would be operating from Troyes, but before I started there I was given one more job to do for H.Q. H.Q., B.A.F.F., was by then anticipating a move from Coulommiers to Orléans in the near future. As I was mobile and knew the country, it was my task to survey an escape route if H.Q. had to move in a hurry. Here and there in the next week or ten days bridges were attacked by the enemy from the air or mined by the French so we had to be sure of a straight run without diversions. This job filled me with some alarm. When the move was to take place, seventy-four vehicles would be involved and, although the route might be negotiable at the time of my investigation, a bridge blown up, a level crossing closed or one direct hit by a bomb on the road could halt the whole procession. I could then imagine the remarks of the top brass. Who the hell suggested *this* route?

Thus, imagining myself to be a convoy of seventy-four vehicles of all weights, I set off from Coulommiers armed with maps and timing every stage on the way. The distance is less than a hundred miles, but it could be a hundred miles of hazards with the Germans behind us. Moreover one had to reckon with concentrations of refugees. I had seen in the north what chaos that could cause. In the end it was the refugees on the roads which went a long way towards losing the war. They impeded troop movements and generally caused panic and confusion. This was of course just what the Germans planned and their bombing and machine-gunning of the roads was done to create as much havoc as possible.

The working out of a route involved level crossings, railway bridges, the crossing of the Seine and the Yonne and one single-line traffic bridge. There was also the problem of permissible weights on bridges. Eventually I worked out a way avoiding some of the obvious main roads which, as I found later, refugees tended to use. I returned over the same route, checking as I went, and handed in my recommendation, which was through Chailly-en-Brie, St Just, Châteaubleau, Maison Rouge, Donnemarie-en-Montois (delightful name), Chatenay sur Seine, Montereau, Nemours, Beaumont, Bellegarde, Châteauneuf sur Loire and into Orléans from the east. The new H.Q. was to be at Olivet on the Loiret.

On the way down to Orléans I found quite a lot of refugees at Chatenay and more on the road to Montereau. However, Montereau was the best place for crossing the Seine and the Yonne so we had to risk the refugees. The move eventually took place so I assumed that it was without mishap. I would have heard if anything had gone wrong. The only casualty was the rest of my baggage, including my precious camp kit. I had lost one lot in the bombing of Arras, so now I had little more than what I was wearing. I was sorry to lose my Gieves great-coat – they were of much better quality at the beginning of the war than those made later – and my silk dressing gown. When I claimed much later for the loss of my kit, the Air Ministry would not admit a claim for the dressing gown. Officers on active service should not have silk dressing gowns!

I set up my own H.Q. at the Grand Hotel in Troyes though I was to spend the next week or more roaming round the country. I had a long list of crashed aircraft to inspect, as both the Luftwaffe and our A.A.S.F. had been very active. The sad thing about the whole Battle of France was that it was not realized by the troops on the ground how active and overstrained our own air forces were, nor how serious were their losses. In the heroic story of the Dunkirk evacuation much has been written praising the little boats and the yachtsmen and fishermen who manned them, not to mention the contribution of the Royal Navy and the French Navy. And rightly so. But it is not always

realized what an important part the Royal Air Force played in making
the Dunkirk deliverance possible.

The Luftwaffe did everything possible to disrupt the embarkations,
not only in the docks and on the beaches but off-shore. It was the
British Spitfires and Defiants which broke up the enemy formations
and held them off their targets. This often happened inland where the
troops on the ground could not appreciate what had happened. The
Royal Air Force inflicted four times their own losses, showing the
same superior quality they were to demonstrate later in the Battle of
Britain. Yet again and again in our contacts with Army units right up
to our final escape from France, we met the same bitter hostility —
"What's the bloody Air Force supposed to be doing?"

Apart from my activities examining German aircraft, it was decided
that I could be used to spy out the land. We were apparently not well
posted on what the French were up to. I suspect that at times they
were not very sure themselves. I therefore had to contact any French
units in the area up to Rheims and beyond and keep an eye on roads
and bridges. To speed up communications I was provided with a
wireless van in addition to my car. I was also given what were called
psycho cards for a daily change of code. I was to call A.A.S.F.
headquarters at Troyes regularly with any news either on shot-down
aircraft or anything else I could pick up.

So off we went into the pleasant countryside north of Troyes in the
warm summer weather like scouts on a picnic. Curiously enough, I
remember the period from 22nd May to the end of the month as a
time of happy relaxation despite all the *Sturm und Drang* which was
going on not very far from the country we were exploring.

We did one test call from Pont Ste Marie just outside Troyes and
then made our way towards Sézanne through Méry-sur-Seine and
Anglure. Before we left I had a quick look at the little church at Pont
Ste Marie and I was amazed to hear the choir practice going on as if
they had never heard about the war. In those days there was
screaming panic in one place and in another one could enjoy the
measured peace of the Pastoral Symphony in Arcis-sur-Aube while
Vitry-le-François, less than twenty miles away, was bombed flat. Only
the chimney stacks were left standing like a forest built of bricks.

We sent back our signals in the course of our wanderings and then
our radio communication broke down on our third night out at a place
with the strange name of Queudes between Anglure and Sézanne.
While the van went back for repairs, I decided to go up as far as

Rheims and make contact with the French Army there.

Why the French did not have me proscribed as a public nuisance, I shall never know. At all times they were not only helpful but hospitable. God knows they had enough to worry them yet I was always welcomed and given every facility to go anywhere, inspect anything and interrogate anybody. Then the general or the colonel would usually invite me to lunch or dinner. That did not happen at H.Q. Coulommiers. Later, on one occasion when I was posted missing and finally returned, my lowly equals appeared to be delighted to see me again while my superiors merely remarked, "Oh God, have *you* turned up again?"

I think the reason for the cordiality shown me by the French was that I spoke their language and understood what they were talking about. Englishmen who spoke little or no French were inclined to offend or irritate them, to be shy and reserved, and this was at times misinterpreted by the French as rudeness. They were therefore quite relieved when they found a British officer who spoke French and was sympathetic to their way of doing things. There is a story of Sir John French inspecting the defences at Huy (pronounced the same as *Oui*) on the Meuse in the first war. He insisted on pronouncing it as Hoy and then demanded to know why the Germans would be going there. One of the French officers present, irritated by the General's manner, replied – in French – "To go fishing!" This of course had to be covered up by the interpreter. If one is going to adopt the attitude – "Bloody frogs! Why can't they speak English?" one is not going to get much co-operation.

I passed through Sézanne, where there were British and French troops. There I learned that the Marne bridges were wired for mines, which I would have thought was already known by our own army. Still, one never knew. Liaison was not always as good as it might be and I was sometimes thanked for information which I considered a glimpse of the obvious. I examined a Heinkel 111 at Echampeu near Lizy-sur-Ourcq. It had been shot down by A.A. and fighter fire on the 19th. Out of a crew of five, one had died and another was at Meaux with a wounded leg. I could not find out where the others were. However, it was an interesting crash as the aircraft was fitted with a type of bombsight which we had not seen before. In cases like this the French allowed us to go to their aircraft establishment at Orléans-Bricy to examine new types of equipment and to get copies of their reports.

When I arrived in Rheims, I found the town deserted. There is something quite frightening about an abandoned town. First there is the silence and then the feeling that anyone or anything might be hiding round the next corner. One passes street after street without meeting anyone, apart from sentries patrolling here and there. There were notices on the walls marked with a skull and crossbones and the brief announcement – "Looters will be shot at sight!"

There is one unexpected danger in a town which has been evacuated for more than a few days – starving dogs. As soon as we opened the car doors abandoned dogs came up looking unpleasantly hungry. One could not help feeling sorry for them. They were either left behind or, in the case of the farm dogs, tied to the axles of farm carts and dragged, dusty, tired and panting along the roads packed with refugees.

I spent an hour with the *Commandant de Place* at Rheims who gave me his views on the situation and locations of shot-down aircraft. I left Rheims that evening and picked up my radio van again at Moussy, just south of Epernay, where we spent the night.

The next day I went back to Rheims and contacted the staff of Sixth Army H.Q. I had lunch with General Keller and was then allowed to visit the trenches at Neufchâtel sur Aisne, north of Rheims. This is where I walked into the atmosphere of the 1914 war. I was told that there were Germans holding the other side of the Aisne but that there was nothing to worry about as long as you kept your head down. I also heard that there were German tanks up the road towards Laon. This did nothing to make me wish to prolong my stay. Having established that the bridges at Neufchâtel and Berry au Bac had been blown up, I felt more reassured and decided to take my leave.

We spent the night in a wood near Epernay. During the night I was awakened by the sound of distant gunfire accompanied by flashes of light. What was more alarming was that it was to the south, that is to say between us and home! We had a conference and resolved to keep hidden in the wood in case we had been overrun by the enemy. We passed the remainder of the night with little rest and set off again very cautiously as soon as it was light. Nothing was moving on the near-by main road so we ventured to the next village. There I found a peasant going about his early morning work. I asked him if there had been any activity in the night as I had heard gunfire and seen flashes of light. He seemed amused and explained that there is often thunder in the summer at that time and that the flashes I had seen were lightning.

"On the road to Louvain, May 1940" by Edward Ardizzone, then a War Office artist.

Unexpected visitor at RAF Pembrey. Our first intact Fw 190 fighter landed by mistake on a British airfield.

Mussolini asked Hitler if he could be allowed to take part in the air attack on Britain in 1940. Among the few Italian aircraft which appeared over the English coast this Fiat CR 42 was left behind in Suffolk.

Someone later told me that the iron in the ground of that grape-growing country causes flashes of lightning to strike low down on the undulating hills and I had mistaken that for gun flashes or explosions. One more sigh of relief for the tenderfoot!

We went back for a night at Troyes. This town has a reputation for some of the prettiest girls in France. The foreign uniform was again working wonders here. One saw the most gorgeous girls on the arm of some scruffy-looking A.C.2 while French lieutenants fumed at the invasion.

On the subject of girls there was one outstandingly attractive one who used to haunt the "Lion d'Or" at Rheims when it was crowded with young R.A.F. officers of the A.A.S.F. She was more intelligent than the usual run of females one meets in such places. She was not unduly inquisitive but she obviously had her ear to the ground. Then came the move to Troyes and we thought we had seen the last of her until one evening I found her in the bar of the Grand Hotel where I was staying. I asked her what she was doing there and she said she had a job in the bar collecting up glasses. I could only think that, if I were as attractive as she was, I could find a better occupation than that. The proprietor told me that she had no job there but had volunteered to tidy up the bar. I asked her how she knew that we were moving from Rheims to Troyes, as the move was supposed to be secret. She replied that everybody knew and disappeared rather hurriedly. I did not see her again but, when the final move to the coast began, I heard that she had been arrested and shot as a spy.

As the days went by in Troyes, we received increasingly depressing reports from the Dunkirk region. Then, when we had the news of the miraculous deliverance of over three hundred thousand men, now safely back in England, it occurred to us that we were still in France with no miraculous deliverance in sight for us.

IX

As far as I was concerned, there was little time to worry about how we were to get out of France. My diaries at that period do not appear to allow any time for sleep. I travelled all over the area from Troyes northwards and along the line of the Aisne. I was joined at times by my young colleague, Colin Bell. He now helped out with crash inspections and interrogations.

At Château Thierry we called on a French Army unit which was holding the crew of a Heinkel 111 of the Boelcke Geschwader. This aircraft had been shot down at Pont-aux-Dames while on a mission to bomb the railway at Mareuil-sur-Ourcq. It had a crew of five N.C.O.s. Four of them were locked in a W.C. on the edge of what appeared to be a school playground. The French said that they were at our disposal but I had no wish to interrogate them in a W.C., apart from the fact that it held only four standing up. I suggested that they should be let out two at a time so that Bell and I could interrogate one each as we walked round the playground. A French sentry was told off to follow us round.

It may well be imagined that the wretched prisoners were only too glad to be let loose. Apart from the hygienic aspect of housing them in a W.C., it is always a mistake to leave a number of prisoners together. They should be isolated as soon as they are captured and questioned while they are feeling relieved at being alive and possibly nervous about their fate. Once they regain confidence and have a chance of concocting a story among themselves, there is much less hope of getting anything out of them. Information gained from one isolated prisoner can be used to influence another. Some prisoners will talk more freely if they think one has already extracted something from their comrades. It also enables one to spring surprises and to get the reaction, "How do you know all that?" If they think you know most of the story, they may tell you the rest. However, I must say that in general German prisoners behaved correctly. Many steadfastly limited themselves to the regulation name, rank and number.

Different interrogators have different techniques. One officer I knew, when confronted by a prisoner standing stiffly to attention and feeling that he was being very correct, would say, "Why are you standing there like a pregnant lark?" He assured me that this unexpected question usually took the wind out of their sails. Where he learned the expression – a pregnant lark (*eine schwangere Lerche*) – I have no idea. It is not a German idiomatic expression, but I can well imagine that it might take a prisoner by surprise. I found that the most effective approach was to be polite. Many Germans expect one to bellow questions in the German manner or to intimidate them in some way. If one could get them to talk in an everyday conversational tone on general subjects, they were more likely to relax and possibly give themselves away.

I interrogated three of the crew, Bell and I took one together and then he questioned the fifth. One man I handled was the wireless operator, Sergeant P. Tappe. He was twenty-five, unmarried and had been in the Luftwaffe for four years. He gave very little information beyond the location of his unit near Ulm and the target of their mission. But he was quite willing to chat in a friendly way, no doubt to keep out of that W.C. as long as possible, and he volunteered the information that the bridge at La Ferté-sous-Jouarre was to be bombed and that any civilians should be moved away. I gathered later that this unusual piece of intelligence was acted upon by the French.

This particular interrogation had a sequel about a year later. When I returned to London towards the end of June, I went back to my Air Ministry job to examine aircraft shot down in the London Blitz. Early in 1941 I was running through reports on German crews, dead or alive, which were sent to us regularly by the R.A.F. interrogation centre. One report concerned a Heinkel 111 shot down in the Thames in an attack on London. All that was recovered was a body washed up in the estuary. The man's pay-book was in his pocket. He was a wireless operator and his name was Sergeant P. Tappe.

It was one of the terms of the armistice signed at Compiègne on 22nd June 1940 that all prisoners in French hands were to be released and these included 750 Luftwaffe prisoners in France, who should have been handed over to the British and had not been. So Sergeant Tappe had gone back to be killed in a bombing raid on London a year later.

We carried on with our bridge inspections. It seemed a curious occupation for a Royal Air Force officer to travel round finding out if the French were doing their job. But the French did not seem to mind. I went to Châlons-sur-Marne and managed to find five minutes to see the cathedral before I checked that the canal and river bridges had been mined. On the way back I stopped at Vitry-le-François which I had come to know quite well from my earlier visits east to Nancy. It was sad to find it empty and with only its chimney stacks standing after the bombing. One bridge was mined and the other blocked. Two bridges at Pogney between Châlons and Vitry-le-François were simply guarded with Bren guns and a tank. Somehow in all my wanderings I did not get the feeling that the Germans would have any difficulty once they decided to move. I had been exploring in the Rheims-Soissons-Rethel area of the Sixth Army. Apart from a few wires on bridges there was little effort to set up a strong defence line. I saw no tank traps, no extensive trench system except the 1914 set-up at Neufchâtel. Roads were open. One could not say that this was a strongly held line and I made up my mind to be well away from it when the next big move came.

I could detect no very strong feeling of resistance among the French. Much as I admired and still admire the courage of the French soldier, there was none of the spirit of Verdun at that time. The initiative was in the hands of the Germans and one knew they were ready to turn south once the north was cleared up. They would soon be over the Somme and the Aisne while the French Staff were still thinking in the terms of 1918.

On 30th May I paid my last visit to Coulommiers and thence drove to Paris before moving to Orléans, our last H.Q. in France for me. I passed through Vincennes with a stop at H.Q. there and another at the barracks in the Place de la République in Paris. The city had now a deserted and forlorn air as I drove down the Boulevard Diderot to the Pont d'Austerlitz and the Gare d'Orléans. The whole station area, inside and out, was packed with refugees of all classes. There they stood or sat, patiently waiting for trains which would probably never leave. There were whole families in their hundreds surrounded by their baggage and even their bedding. Some even had birds in cages. Men, women and children were weeping. It was an enormous tableau of despair.

There was a lot of road traffic moving southwards and I joined in and drove down the Boulevard de l'Hôpital to the Porte d'Italie. Once outside Paris the situation got worse. The main road from Paris to Orléans was full of refugees on foot, in cars and in horse-drawn vehicles. It would take days to cover what was normally a run of an hour and a half. So we left the main road and found that some of the smaller roads more or less parallel were fairly free. We passed through villages called something or other on the Orge and finally fought our way through another concentration of refugees into Orléans.

The confusion and misery on the roads in that hot summer were increased by the almost complete breakdown of the civilian administration in the towns and villages we passed. Shops were closed. There were no petrol pumps working and no repair garages. There was no medical care and wherever refugee centres had been set up, they were soon overwhelmed. As the panic grew, more and more abandoned their homes. Whole towns and villages emptied. Farms were left with the crops growing and the animals untended.

Sometimes troops had to fight their way against the stream of refugees and they were finally mixed up with stragglers from the armies who had joined the rush southwards. Here and there by the roadside, whole fields were filled with exhausted people taking a hurried meal – if they had anything to eat. At one such halt, a little girl came and watched us unpacking our sandwiches and chocolate ration. Who can eat in that situation? So she got the lot and rushed off joyfully to her family.

And over it all was the threat of the German dive-bomber. To the enemy throughout the campaign the fleeing population afforded a great advantage by disorganizing communications and troop movements. Well might the Germans have taken their text from Milton –

> With ruin upon ruin, rout on rout,
> Confusion worse confounded.

It served them well. Yet, in August 1940 in a French edition of *Signal*, a German propaganda magazine, the blame for the plight of the refugees was put on the French authorities, "who deliberately encouraged this mad panic". Who was it, the writer asked, who brought the first succour to the poor people on the roads? Why, the German troops, of course! This was accompanied by pictures of peasants weeping and two exhausted old women by the roadside, "chased from their homes by unscrupulous French propaganda".

In the same number of the magazine was a series of photographs of German troops with flame-throwers burning out the occupants of pill-boxes in the Maginot Line.

X

It was 31st May when I arrived in Orléans. The Dunkirk evacuation was well under way but we had no orders to get out. In fact for the following ten days I had a full programme of work. I spent three days at Nogent, operating from there and doing a liaison job with the French. I also had to visit the French Centre d'Essais examining German aircraft which had been brought in for investigation.

I was sending in scraps of paper removed from aircraft and prisoners "which might be of interest", drawings of squadron badges from aircraft and any odds and ends of equipment which I could get out of the French. The Germans were increasing the number of machine guns carried on bombers. They must have been finding that our fighters were doing a lot of damage, as they began to install fairly heavy armour plate to protect the pilot and other members of the crew. Most of the crashed aircraft I examined were a week or more old and prisoners had been dispersed. It is surprising that I found time to write quite a number of letters home in those early days of June and even more so to find later that they had all arrived. It was only towards the end of the second week of June that the postal service broke down.

Although some roads north from Orléans were now clear of refugees, travel was difficult owing to the convoys going up to the front. Returning from French Air H.Q., I met a fast-moving convoy near Melun. As we were passing it, one lorry swung out of line and tore both offside doors from my car. Fortunately both my driver and I were on the nearside. In such circumstances one cannot call a policeman nor can one stop a convoy on the way to the front. We limped on till we came to a level crossing, where the crossing-keeper's wife cleaned up our cuts, gave us a drink and sent us on our way with the left side of the car wide open. This was of course a motorized convoy but at many other places it was interesting to see how much horses and mules were still being used. This was also true of the German supply lines.

I had one very pleasant encounter with the Senior Air Staff Officer, Air Vice-Marshal Evill, who received my situation report as if it were of some value. I also had to report to our Army Intelligence, though I doubt if my scraps of information were of much use in all that confusion. My brief in general was to speed up any kind of intelligence, not to waste time on individual aircraft in remote places and to get hold of prisoners if possible.

My impression of those first ten days of June is one of almost complete confusion. I rushed to and fro between Nogent and Orléans and travelled round the country towards Paris and Troyes. No one knew anything and I more often found that I was asked for information rather than receiving it. Dunkirk was now over and I was amazed to learn that there were over a hundred thousand of us still in France. I was optimistic enough to think that H.Q. Staff would be flown out but in the end it was a matter – at least at my level – of *sauve qui peut*.

On 5th June came the news of the beginning of the final Battle of France. The Germans crossed the Somme accompanied by a gigantic bombardment from the sea to Laon, north-west of Rheims. It was then that the French fought hard, but the situation reports became worse and worse. When, four days later, the Germans attacked on the Aisne front, the whole line across France was in movement with the French falling back in disorder and despair. German tanks and dive-bombers seemed to go where they liked. Most of the towns I had operated from were now in enemy hands. Germans would soon be drinking up our champagne in Rheims. The fall of Paris was imminent. French H.Q. at La Ferté was abandoned for Briare in the Loire department.

The exodus from Paris was increasing. In a few days over a million Parisians had left. Even a declaration that Paris was an open city did not deter people from setting out on a hopeless trek. On 10th June Italy declared war. The jackal had joined the hyena and wanted its share of the pickings. This news coupled with the feeble Italian invasion of France caused a rush of refugees from the south. Eventually they met those from the north. Some from the south even got as far as Orléans, which only added to our difficulties. One can imagine what it meant to the unfortunate refugees.

About this time, I had been out in the country for some days. I heard later that I had been counted as missing. In one abandoned office – I have no idea where it was – I found a field telephone still in working order. I knew that by now my family would be worrying, as I had not come out at Dunkirk, and I felt sure that letters were not getting through. There was still a telephone connection between Paris and London but it was obviously strictly limited to matters of the highest priority. If I used it, I might be breaking in on a conversation between Churchill and Reynaud. However, I decided to risk it. I picked up the receiver and in my most official voice demanded "Table A, Paris". I knew that this was the link as I had heard the top brass using it. I expected to be challenged on my identity and authority but to my surprise I was put through at once. When they replied, I asked, still with my Air Marshal's voice, for Air Ministry, London, hoping to God that I would not be put on to the Chief of Air Staff or the Minister himself. Air Ministry replied at once and I asked for the Duty Officer, praying that it would be someone I knew. It was. Robin Steele, a first war veteran and a colleague in my own section, was on the line. In about thirty seconds I gave him my wife's telephone number to ring and say he had heard from me. This I know he did in the following few minutes. I did not attempt to explain what I had done. I just dropped the receiver and fled as far from that telephone as possible. On retrospect, I am horrified to think that, out of over a hundred thousand of us still in France, I had the nerve to ring through to my wife on a line which at that time must have been red hot. It is the element of surprise which matters. No one on Table A in Paris would have imagined that a very junior officer would ring up his wife with the Germans at the gates of Paris and France almost at the moment of collapse.

The French were now retiring across the Marne, the last bastion which had been saved by Gallieni's troops in Paris taxis at the beginning of the 1914 war. Paris had held out for four years then. This time it would fall within a little over four weeks of the German invasion.

Now that I have grown older and, I hope, a little wiser, I have often thought of those soldiers in the Maginot Line and particularly of the Arabs, Senegalese and Indo-Chinese troops who had been shipped thousands of miles from their homes and families to help white men fight white men. It is all very well to laugh at the simple black soldier who was fooled by an insurance policy with a big red seal on it. How much of his language do I understand? I could not help wondering

then what went on in the minds of those colonial troops. Were the
meagre pay and inadequate rations sufficient to explain their presence
there? Colonial troops had fought in the Crimea, in the Franco-
Prussian War, in 1914–18 and here they were again. I doubt if they
would have made much of the Ems telegram or the murder of the
Archduke Francis Ferdinand or the wrongs of Poland. I once saw in
the churchyard of a small Belgian village the graves of half a dozen
Arab soldiers. They seemed strangely out of place and a long way
from Mecca. Still, my own brother lies on a remote Burmese hillside
with no better reason and to no good purpose either.

I have tried to give some idea of the human misery I saw in France
on the roads in 1940. I saw the same agony on the roads in 1945 and
this time they were Germans. On one occasion I was at the Silesian
Station in Berlin. There the fleeing multitudes were coming in, this
time on trains from East Prussia, packed like cattle inside or hanging
on anywhere outside. To their misery and despair was added
starvation. Little people who had been driven from their homes
carrying only the barest necessities. Belgians, French, Germans, I
found, were all the same. German children cry in the same way as
Belgian and French children and they are just as hungry and tired.

As the end drew near in France, the Entente Cordiale died at all
levels. The French, earlier on so friendly, now began to turn on us
when they saw our preparations for departure. It seemed much longer
than a few months since we were welcomed as allies and conquering
heroes. There was still a feeling of comradeship on the part of the
French troops but the refugees and the people in the villages through
which we passed were openly hostile. They knew we were on the run.
Some took us for Germans on account of our blue uniforms. Thus we
could hope for no help or sustenance. We were on our own. For me
this was particularly saddening since, from my student days, I had
found the French to be so welcoming and kind. I fear that feeling for
us has never come back. In 1940 we were abandoning them and they
knew it.

I asked if there were any aircraft available to get us back and I was
simply told to make for the coast. Fortunately I still had a car and a
driver. However, before I could leave France, I had to have a
document with my name on it, stating that the above named officer
was now surplus to the establishment of H.Q. Air Component (South)
and had been instructed to report to H.Q. No. 2 Base Area for onward
transmission to the United Kingdom. I was also given an embarkation

order, without which I would not be allowed on board. Without such authorities, I was told, I would be a deserter.

Though I had been retreating for some weeks, I had had a job to do. I belonged to a Headquarters Staff to which I had to report. I could eat regularly in a mess and I had somewhere to sleep. It is true I had had to move house all the way down from Brussels to Orléans, but that was not running away. It was merely keeping out of the enemy's reach. Now, for the first time, I felt I was on the run. After my last mess dinner, I walked out into the darkness wondering what to do next.

I had been brought to the dinner by Squadron Leader Heaton-Armstrong, who struck me as a very unusual Royal Air Force officer. He must have been in his early fifties, he limped badly and was partly blind. Apart from a pair of spectacles, he wore what looked like a small telescope and a monocle round his neck. Yet with all these disabilities he took me under his wing, driving me to the mess in a car specially adapted for his crippled leg. He took me over again as I stood, rather undecided, after dinner. All he asked me to do was to stick my head out of the car window and guide him to a farmhouse where he knew we could spend the night. As it was pitch dark and the car lights had to be dimmed, I did not feel very happy with a partly blind driver with one useless leg. But he was wonderfully patient and confident, driving very slowly and reacting to my rather vague directions. He seemed to know where the place was and eventually we reached a kind of barn at one end of which a short flight of steps led up to a bedroom, furnished with a large bed and an enormous grandfather clock. There was also a settee and a few chairs. I had great difficulty in getting the Squadron Leader up the steps and finally into bed. Once he was settled, I lay down on the settee and tried to sleep.

Despite the good dinner, I found it hard to get to sleep. The Squadron Leader was disturbed by the ticking of the great clock, so I had to get up and stop it. Then, in the middle of the night, he was seized with cramp, as he could rest only in one position on account of his leg. I got up again and eased him into a more comfortable position, after which we both slept till morning. I had to get him down the steps again and we set off back to what was left of H.Q. There I took leave of him. I heard later that he had been flown back to England. I found my own driver with my car and, with a stock of petrol on board, we started for the Bay of Biscay.

Many years later, I was walking across St James's Park to my club when I saw a limping, rather military-looking figure going in the same direction. He was wearing a bowler hat and overcoat but the monocle and the little telescope were still there round his neck. It was Squadron Leader Heaton-Armstrong. I walked with him through the park and we promised to meet again for lunch one day, but we never did. It was only a short time afterwards that I realized that my strange companion on that night in 1940 was Sir John Heaton-Armstrong, Clarenceux King of Arms. I believe he was Chester Herald in the hierarchy of the College of Arms when we met in France, though all I could think of at that time was how a man as disabled as he was could be a R.A.F. officer on active service. The answer was – courage. He had served in the 20th Deccan Horse in France in 1914 and was seriously wounded, losing the sight of one eye and the use of a leg. These injuries he incurred in a hand-to-hand encounter with the enemy, from which he fought his way out with his sword though entirely surrounded. He came to the College of Arms after the war in 1922 as Rouge Dragon Pursuivant of Arms and there he remained for forty-five years, save for the period when he became a R.A.F. intelligence officer. He was also Inspector of Badges of the R.A.F. and many other Commonwealth Air Forces and his signature is on all the squadron badges on the wall of the Royal Air Force Club. I have always remembered his kindness and advice to me on that lonely night in France in 1940. At that time I had left him with some misgiving, wondering how he was going to get back to England. Nevertheless he got away from the Germans for the second time. He was seventy-nine when he died in 1967.

XI

The map of the German advance at that time shows an ever widening cascade of arrows reaching out to the Brittany coast in the west, towards Nantes, Poitiers and Lyon in the south-west and south and to Belfort and Annecy in the south-east. The list of possible exit ports was rapidly running out, even if we could get to the coast. We knew that troops had been embarking at Le Havre, Brest and Cherbourg but we did not know how long that would go on. I therefore decided to make for Nantes which I understood was still a base area.

It was a relief to get away from Orléans, which on 15th June was crowded with refugees from Paris, army stragglers and looters. The panic had increased with the news that Italian fighters and bombers had been attacking bridges and columns of refugees along the Upper Loire. One of the achievements of Mussolini's heroes was to set on fire a hospice at Gien, causing the nuns and the patients to take to the road in the wake of a crowd of children from the nursery school at Montreuil. At the same time the Germans were pressing down relentlessly to the Loire, adding to the terror and confusion. I heard that the bridge at Gien had been blown up on the 16th while it was packed with civilians. Yet when the Germans reached Orléans on the 16th they found the main bridge intact. This enabled them to press on with little resistance from the French to Bourges.

Thus I was very fortunate to be on my way, armed with my two bits of paper authorizing me to leave France and with no other obligation than to get to the coast as soon as I could. My only fear was that we might be cut off by the German advance in the direction of Le Mans, which I was making for. It was a drive through chaos, rumours, misdirections, panic and refugees. From Le Mans I drove on to Angers. There was an air raid while we were in Angers, which gave us even less reason to halt there, so we pressed on to Nantes.

Considering that the Germans were on our heels, I found the camp at Nantes surprisingly well organized. I had imagined that the top brass from our H.Q. would have flown back to England, but Air Marshal Barratt was still at Nantes and getting worried that R.A.F. personnel was not getting away quickly enough.

I was assigned to a place in a tent and told to dump my car for destruction. This was a sad moment. Clearly I could not take it with me and we did not want to make a present of it to the Germans. It was like the Arab's farewell to his steed. That car had carried me out of a lot of trouble. My faithful driver too. In those days I did not drive a car and in any case officers had to be driven. I have therefore a great debt of gratitude to my drivers – Turkington, "Nick" Carter, Allum and many others, who in the past three months had driven me all over France at all hours, had found their way out of every kind of jam, scrounged food and petrol, carried out running repairs, made tea in pouring rain, crawled over and into wrecked aircraft with me and patiently borne with me when I insisted on going off the route to visit churches, cathedrals, châteaux and other tourist landmarks.

I slept the night at Nantes and the next morning I was summoned by a wing commander. I was given charge of a hundred and fifty men ,and a corporal and told to get them to St Nazaire – on foot! Never having had any square-bashing training, I had not the least idea of getting them into any kind of order, but my corporal knew the drill, lined them up and off we marched towards St Nazaire.

Each man carried his kitbag on his shoulder. I had almost no baggage, as most of my kit had been captured. However, I did have a German parachute, which had been presented to me by a French officer, and one of the men volunteered to carry it for me. The men seemed unduly heavily laden and it was explained to me that, when an Army or R.A.F. unit was abandoned, the NAAFI was thrown open and a free-for-all declared. The curious thing was that the men stocked up with large tins of fruit salad and juices and other groceries, quite a burden on that hot June day.

On the road to St Nazaire we had to pass a number of Army units resting by the roadside. They were definitely hostile. Over the past few weeks the R.A.F. had been continually accused of leaving the Army in the lurch. What the Army or at least the lower ranks did not know was that the R.A.F. in France had been stretched to the utmost, often with considerable losses, in support of the Army and not least in the evacuation at Dunkirk. But, because the Army did not always see our aircraft in action, we were reproached for not supplying air cover when it was needed. Now the Army had an opportunity of expressing its disapproval of the R.A.F. as represented by my mobile wholesale grocery unit. It was catcalls most of the way. "Here's the bloody R.A.F. at last!" and "What price Fred Karno's Army!" were among the more flattering remarks. Here and there it looked almost as if it might develop into a fight, so I passed the word down the ranks, "Eyes front and not a word out of any of you!" We had enough worry on our hands without a civil war on foreign territory.

It was evening when we drew near to St Nazaire. From where we were it looked as if an air attack was on so I decided to spend the night on an abandoned airfield. It was better than being bombed in St Nazaire and the men were dead tired. There were still plenty of troops behind us so we were not likely to miss the boat. Had I known then how close the Germans were, I would probably have pressed on. We had no food, save for the stock of tinned groceries, and no water. Then someone found a temporary tap where some building had been going on. The water was not particularly clean but was drinkable. For a nightcap the corporal had a bright idea. Everyone who had a bar of chocolate – and there was one bar in every packet of iron rations, if you had any – was invited to contribute it to a stew of cement and water in an old petrol drum. A fire was lit under it and the bars of chocolate were thrown into the whitish water. The resulting mess boiled up into a faint imitation of cocoa. I was honoured with the first cup. As I did not fall writhing in agony, there was a general distribution and we all retired to rest, except for a couple of sentries, on the very hard concrete in one of the hangars. It was to be my last night's sleep in France. Almost three months to the day had passed since I arrived at Le Havre and it was little more than a month since the Germans had invaded Belgium. While we had been marching up the road the German 33rd Division had entered Orléans. General von Bock was there on the following day. He found a long line of French troop-trains loaded with batteries and ammunition, supply trains and columns of prisoners and refugees. He described it as "a complete picture of a break-down". But the Germans by that time were already advancing on Bourges to the south as indeed they were towards St Nazaire.

In the morning we marched into St Nazaire and on to a quay by one of the shipyards, expecting to see a transport with steam up ready to take us back to England. The quay was empty. There was not even a rowing boat in sight. Amid the usual ribald remarks with which the

British greet such an occasion, we sat down among the kitbags trying to look cheerful. Someone found a hammer and the first hour was passed agreeably with the men making dents in their tin helmets to show that they had been in action. I wandered off round the shipyard looking for some food. I found a canteen but there was nothing to spare. One shipyard worker gave me a cold pork chop which was the equivalent of five loaves and two fishes for my multitude. I was surprised to see that work was still going on in the shipyards although German reconnaissance aircraft appeared from time to time while we were there. In fact, as I heard afterwards, the battleship *Jean Bart* was under construction in the naval dockyard at that time.

I returned to my flock and sat down on the quay, resigned to being a prisoner of war. It was 17th June, the date afterwards announced with the brief statement – Evacuation of the B.E.F. from France completed.

I was thinking rather bitterly that I had managed to get out of Brussels when the Germans were actually there, I had narrowly escaped being killed at Arras, I had been in Amiens, Rheims, Paris, Troyes and Orléans shortly before the Germans arrived and I had finally got to the coast only to have to sit down and wait till the first panzers drove in. Soon I would have to tell the men that there was no hope of being taken off and nowhere else to run to. Up till then, I had not shared my misgivings with the men, who usually rely on an officer to know more than they do. I began to wonder when the aircraft droning high overhead would start dropping their loads when a destroyer appeared. It was *Havock*, which had come down from Narvik. She still had her arctic camouflage.

She tied up right in front of us and an officer told me we would be going aboard at once but that no kit could be carried. So I gave the order to pile kitbags and threw my own small bag down on the heap. The men were naturally disappointed that they were not to be permitted to take home the groceries they had dragged all the way from Nantes, but that was nothing against the prospect of getting home at last. So with other units which had come up we clambered on to the destroyer till we were packed chest to chest. There is not much in the way of a rail round a destroyer and we had to hang on to one another as she got under way.

Once out of the estuary I found we were making for two large liners which were lying out in the bay. Our destination was *Duchess of York*, a Canadian Pacific passenger ship of about 20,000 tons. The White

A Ju 88 makes a forced landing on Oakington aerodrome.

After lifting and getting the undercarriage down . . .

. . . the German bomber is wheeled into a hangar, Wing Commander
'Sailor' Malan in the cockpit.

All that was left of a Ju 88 shot down near Aston Down, Cirencester.

My WAAF driver helps the war economy by siphoning some high octane petrol into my car from the tank of a Heinkel III shot down near Honiton, Devon.

Star liner *Georgic* was also standing by a short way off. Our destroyer drew alongside *Duchess of York* and a plank, which looked to me about six inches wide, was thrown across from the destroyer's deck into a small door halfway down the ship. A more precarious bridge could hardly be imagined. Fortunately the water was as smooth as the Serpentine, my favourite waterway.

The men started to run across. Heroically I stood back until the corporal and all my men were over. The truth is that I was scared and had left the ordeal to the very last moment. I have a horror of heights. I have flown round the world many times at all heights without any worry but halfway up a ladder my knees begin to dissolve. However, there were still crowds behind me and over I went, gratefully falling into the bowels of *Duchess of York*. One of the men had carried my German parachute. That was allowed as a valuable piece of enemy equipment. Valuable it was indeed. It furnished my small daughter with nightdresses, petticoats and pants throughout most of the clothes rationing period in England.

I do not know how many thousand men were finally packed into that ship, as it was almost impossible to move on board. I went up on deck just in time to see *Georgic* obscured from view by the splash caused by a bomb dropped between the two ships. No one seemed to worry. What mattered was that we had a ship under our feet. Yet it was about that time that the *Lancastria* was sunk in Quiberon Bay. I was told that of about 6,000 men, 4,000 were lost on board or drowned in the oil-covered sea. Churchill withheld the news of that frightful disaster, the worst of the whole evacuation. He said there was enough bad news then for the public to take.

Soon after we were loaded and in the general struggle for breathing space below, I made the acquaintances of the purser of the ship. He invited me into his cabin. "What you need," said he, "is a drop of Nelson's Blood!" That was my first introduction to the mixture which kept me in a state of moderate intoxication until we reached England. While I was sitting in his cabin with the first dose in my hand, there was a shattering crash which shook the whole ship. I realized that I had come all this way only to find a watery grave. Truly cowards die many times before their death. "Depth charge!" said my friend the purser and poured himself another drink.

A Sunderland flying boat accompanied us for the first hour and then left us on our own. I asked what port we were going to. Apparently all the ports on the south coast were full of shipping and we were destined for Liverpool. So we zigzagged up the Irish Sea for two days to avoid submarines and at long last came into the Mersey estuary. On the way up to the pierhead we passed wrecks sunk by mines and then before us appeared what seemed to me then to be the most beautiful piece of architecture in the world, the Royal Liver Building.

I had had a wash and shave to shake off to some extent the effect of Nelson's Blood and I had seen to it that my men had polished their buttons. Somehow they too had managed to shave. I told them that we were part of one of the greatest retreats in history but that we did not need to look the part. They lined up very smartly on the quay and we marched off to the railway station. That night we arrived at Bridgnorth in Shropshire. Three days later, on 22nd June, the French delegates signed the armistice terms in Foch's railway carriage at Compiègne. They then left for Rome for the even more humiliating ceremony of signing the armistice with Italy. The Battle of France was over. It had cost France 100,000 dead, 120,000 wounded and a million and a half prisoners.

PART II

Picking up the Pieces

A surprise visitor to Scotland

XII

It is not for me to write an inquest on the Fall of France. Many hands more skilled than mine have done that. But, as I looked back on the events of the previous three months from the comparative safety of my own country, I could not help feeling that, had the French been competently led by generals who understood this new kind of warfare and had the politics at the top been less murky, the Fall of France need not have happened. Whilst reluctantly giving the Germans the credit for a classic victory, one can only agree with Sir Basil Liddell Hart that "never was a great disaster more easily preventable". What does seem incredible, forty years after, is that the French sat there on the defensive – and not a very efficient defence at that – throughout the phoney war, leaving the initiative entirely to the enemy. There was never any question of attack. Foch once said, "My centre is giving way, my right is in retreat; situation excellent. I shall attack." In 1940 we never heard the word except when it was applied to the enemy's activities.

I was surprised when 25th June was proclaimed a day of national mourning by the French government. Mourning for what? Their own incompetence? The French people and the hundreds of thousands of refugees had had enough mourning already while every officer and soldier must have felt bewildered and humiliated. General Weygand that day issued his last Order to the French Army:

> The fortune of war has gone against us, but at least you responded magnificently to the appeals I addressed to your patriotism, your bravery and your tenacity ... Remain united and trust your leaders ... Keep up your spirits, my friends.
> *Vive la France.*

General Weygand, it must be admitted, had the misfortune to be called upon to command an army which was already beaten, but I doubt if his last Order commanded much respect. Trust your leaders, forsooth! That was the final irony.

I felt very sad, sad for the proud French people, for the dead and for all those men who were now prisoners of war. At the same time I had a feeling of relief and gratitude to our own people, especially the Royal Navy, who had brought us safely out of what was to be four years of darkness over Europe.

I now had my own men to look after and see them settled. I gathered that Bridgnorth was a centre for re-distributing the miscellaneous collection of men from all units who had come out in the general scramble from France. Then I began to wonder what was going to happen to me. I had been a member of the staff of H.Q., B.A.F.F., which now no longer existed. I realized that I was *en disponibilité*, which is a bad thing to be. From the beginning a faulty left eye had precluded flying duties, so that I might well get a chairborne posting as an adjutant on some remote station in the marsh somewhere or given the task of counting stores of boots in the Equipment Branch. It was a moment for action before anyone had any bright ideas about my future. Thus I presented myself before the C.O. and explained that I had to report back to the Air Ministry on my activities in France. It is true that I had gained in those three months more experience in examining crashed German aircraft than my former colleagues in England simply because shot-down aircraft were far more plentiful in France. I had also gathered a good deal of information which could still be operationally useful. Once back at the Air Ministry, I knew that I would probably be received back into the bosom of A.C.A.S. (I). I made no mention of my natural desire to get to London to see my family nor of my reluctance to take on a dogsbody's job in the Outer Hebrides. The C.O. readily agreed that I should proceed to London at once, probably because I would be one problem less. A body of men would be leaving for Uxbridge the next day and I would be in charge of them. After that I could report to the Air Ministry.

That piece of diplomacy concluded, I tried in vain to borrow a shirt. I had been wearing an airman's shirt for longer than I could remember and it was hardly sanitary. I just had to set off with what I stood up in and hope that no one would stand very close to me. With the men I took the train to Euston, whence we marched to Warren Street tube station. I announced to the ticket collector that we were the last of the B.E.F. from France and we were allowed through without tickets. At the depot at Uxbridge I lined them up, made sure they had beds and took leave of them. The next move was to get a few days off to spend with my family. I was received by the officer concerned rather like Oliver Twist before Mr Bumble. "Leave? Don't you know there's a war on?" "Yes," I replied heroically, "I've just been in one." This witty remark was not appreciated. Nevertheless I got two days. When I arrived home, the first thing my wife suggested was a bath, which I badly needed.

As I had hoped, I was put back on the strength of A.I.1(g) and later promoted to the glory of Flight Lieutenant. A number of branches of the Air Ministry, including my own, were at that time located in an infants' school at Harrow Weald. A.I.1(g) was made up of a score of officers under a Squadron Leader C.O., all on call at a moment's notice to go off to crashes anywhere in the country. We had a representative officer at various R.A.F. Maintenance Units from Scotland to Kent whose activities were usually confined to the area covered by the Maintenance Units. Attached to us were three civilian draughtsmen, a number of R.A.F. drivers, WAAFs and a few permanent civil servants. The civil servants' primary duty was to make tea. They also kept the files, instructed us in the arts of making out claim forms for pay and expenses and, as far as the female members were concerned, held off the advances of the more amorous officers.

We had begun to collect quantities of equipment salvaged from German aircraft for study and instruction. This later became a large museum under my curatorship. When we came to amass samples of Lueger pistols, machine-guns and 20 mm. cannon as well as ammunition and bomb fuses, it was a highly dangerous occupation. Like the people who are never happy unless they are messing about in boats, there is a type which cannot keep its hands off firearms and explosives. When we had any of those about, it was best to leave them to it. Instead of leaving any investigation to the people at the Ordnance Board or at Woolwich, one or two of our gun-slinging enthusiasts were in the habit of screwing machine-gun bullets or cannon shells in a vice and carrying out their own private examinations. There must be a special guardian angel for lunatics of this kind since none of them had their heads blown off.

We also accumulated a gruesome wardrobe of flying clothing and helmets from dead crews. After a few days these gave off a frightful smell and the cupboard had to be kept tightly closed. German flying boots were in great demand and eventually we each acquired a pair for use when we were examining crashes in remote parts of the country in the winter.

Up to the time I arrived back in A.I.1(g), German crashes had not been numerous. There had been a few He 111s and Ju 88s and one rare bird in the shape of a Heinkel 115 float seaplane. However, within a fortnight the Battle of Britain was to begin. Picking up the pieces then became a full-time occupation.

I now had no more interrogations to do. We had a close liaison with A.I.1(k), another branch of the Air Ministry, which was staffed with German-speaking officers. They took over survivors from German crashes, leaving the debris to us. We received copies of their interrogations and we supplied them with our crash reports.

In time we thus built up a lot of information on the German Air Force, its order of battle, personnel and equipment. Much of the intelligence we acquired was of immediate operational interest such as strength of units, aircraft performances, location and type of armament, armour protection for crews, radar and radio installations, sizes of bombs and their fuses and anything else likely to be of use to our own fighters and bombers. We also accumulated a dictionary of Luftwaffe slang. Code names had to be identified too. The strips of light metal which we dropped from our bombers to confuse German radar were known on our side as "Window". The Germans called these reflectors "Düppel".

By the time I rejoined A.I.1(g) many more crash officers had been recruited. In our whole unit there was only one regular officer, Squadron Leader Easton, later Air Commodore Sir James Easton, who was our founder C.O. The rest were a mixed bag. We had a mining engineer, two garage proprietors, an aeronautical journalist, a patent agent, an Antwerp merchant, a Woolworth manager, the younger brother of an Irish peer, an official from the Bank of England, a Hampshire J.P., a steel tycoon, the son of a Russian general of the Tsarist days, a scion of an ancient Polish/Lithuanian family who brought his own Rolls Royce, a very senior Army officer from the 1914 war and now a flight lieutenant who used to entertain us at Boodle's, various business men, farmers and others whose origins were never known. A delightful Evelyn Waugh touch was introduced by the presence of Captain Sumner, a civilian employee of the Air Ministry, who had served in the Royal Flying Corps. His subject was balloons. He knew nothing of superchargers on Jumo engines or direct fuel injection but he was useful in steering us through the intricacies of Civil Service life.

Some officers provided their own cars; for all the others there were official cars with WAAF drivers. We all carried cameras, a pair of gum boots and had a small bag of travel kit ready for departure at any hour of the day or night. Though we were supposed to keep normal office hours, varied with periods of night duty, we were on call like doctors for twenty-four hours. At home we frequently had telephone calls in the early hours of the morning – Heinkel down at such and such map reference. The car will pick you up in a quarter of an hour. It was our job to get there as soon as possible. Getting through and out of London in an air raid was the great problem. Roads were blocked and we had to find our way in the dark. Once outside London we had to travel without the benefit of road signs, which had all been removed in the invasion precautions. At times I found myself steering by the sun. Map references were often vague and enemy aircraft came down in the most unlikely places.

I remember leaving London in the midst of one of the worst air raids. All hell seemed let loose overhead. Several times the car seemed to jump as bombs fell close by. Here and there we had to drive over glass or fallen debris or through water from burst mains. I told my WAAF driver to put on her steel helmet but she did not want to spoil her coiffure. So I felt I could not wear mine. Finally we were out beyond Barnet and, as we went north, the lights in the sky faded to a blur on the horizon to the south and the noise fell away to a distant rumble. The moon suddenly came out and we drove on in quite incredible peace. On another occasion I had to spend a night in Cambridge, where I had been stationed for a week or two at the beginning of the war to examine crashes or anything else which fell out of the sky in East Anglia. We had had no sleep or rest for several nights in London. It seemed as if air raids had always been going on and would go on till the end of time. In Cambridge I found a little bedroom near the Silver Street bridge with a view of the Backs. With its sweet-smelling linen and chintz it did not belong to our world. It was so quiet I could not sleep. I lay there and thought of the concrete on which we had slept near St Nazaire and I was grateful that I had been preserved, if only to spend just one night like this in my own country with the scent of the summer flowers just outside my window.

For a time our unit overflowed into the office of the Charity Commissioners at the corner of Ryder Street in St James's. By some curious twist of the official mind, exile from Harrow Weald to the temptations of the big city entitled us to an extra allowance. Among the more unusual jobs of the Night Duty Officer at Ryder Street – and we all had to take our turn – was the inspection of the roof for parachutists. A sentry stood up there on the parapet and we had to make sure he was there. My standing orders were, in the event of an attack by the enemy, to destroy him. Failing this, I had to telephone Wellington Barracks and they would arrange to do the job. Happily this desperate situation did not arise.

In our various offices "flap-meters" were in operation. These were analogous to the Beaufort Scale of wind force. The degree of flap among more excitable officers ranged from "The P.M. wants to know" down through such alarms as "The Chief Constable of Suffolk has a piece of a sewing machine which was dropped from the sky during an air raid" to "Miss Mapleson forgot to buy any tea". The usual cause of a flap would be an urgent telephone call for information which we could not immediately supply or for a piece of enemy equipment which we did not happen to have in stock. The various experts on this or that subject would go into frenzied action with slide rules and dictionaries and the arrow on the flap-meter would rise in accordance with the degree of eminence of the enquirer. One flap had a most tragic ending. We received a message from the Ministry of Aircraft Production that they needed a specimen of a particular German bomb fuse. It was called a "50" fuse and it incorporated an anti-interference device. It so happened that a large bomb fitted with this fuse had fallen at Biggin Hill and had not exploded. One of our officers had begun to specialize in bombs and fuses, although there were bomb-disposal squads all over the country to deal with U.X.B.s as they were called, so off he went to Biggin Hill. He was warned to use a remote-control apparatus. However, he decided to do the job manually and was blown up, not before he had sent his assistant back out of range.

I cannot imagine greater courage than that of the man who goes out alone to investigate and defuse a bomb or a mine with a telephone slung round his neck, coolly explaining step by step what he is doing in case he makes a wrong move and blows himself up. Towards the beginning of the war, Lieutenant-Commander Ouvry did such a job on the first magnetic mine. I had occasion to investigate with him a German float seaplane, which had come ashore at Sheringham in Norfolk. It was thought that it might have been carrying a magnetic mine. Fortunately it wasn't or I would have retired to King's Lynn. I once had to take an unexploded butterfly bomb from Harrow to Woolwich and that was quite enough for me. Some of the unexploded bombs dropped on London were taken out to Richmond Park, where I saw a number of them laid out by some wooden huts. A day or two later the whole lot blew up. I decided thereafter to keep to my own modest speciality which covered German military terms and abbreviations.

I had just time enough to settle in with the new boys when the Battle of Britain opened on 10th July. The story of the part our fighters played has been written and will never be forgotten. This is the story of the humbler brethren on the ground who picked up the pieces.

XIII

From the first week in July 1940 till the middle of September the fate of this country hung in the balance, but our chances of survival, which God knows varied enough throughout the war, were never lower than in those few weeks after the return from France. We may have saved most of our army but our losses in material had been enormous. Moreover we had precious little in stock to replace those losses.

The Royal Air Force had been hard hit in France and Fighter Command was reduced to just over 300 Hurricanes and Spitfires after Dunkirk. By an incredible boost in production this figure was more than doubled in six weeks but it was still far from what was needed to hold the Luftwaffe off. On the other hand our radar network could to some extent balance lack of numbers and ensure that our aircraft were in the right place at the right time. The desperate shortage of equipment for the ground forces at that time meant that the army was ill prepared to repel an invasion. It was therefore all the more important that the R.A.F. should hold out, because for the Germans victory in the air was the pre-requisite to the assault on our shores.

Fortunately for us the Germans were rather haphazard in their bombing attacks. They had several purposes, none of which they fully accomplished. Their changes of tactics were · frequently to our advantage. At one time, when they had seriously disorganized our air control system, they suddenly turned their attention to London as a target and gave us a much needed breathing space to get our communications working again.

Six years later, I had the opportunity of discussing German bombing strategy with Albert Speer at the Nuremberg trials. I have always been of the opinion that the Germans could have done the maximum damage to our aircraft production by concentrating their attacks on our few propeller factories. You can have all the aircraft and pilots but they are useless without propellers. It was our heel of

Achilles. I suggested to Speer that, if they had gone for those propeller plants instead of bombing the so-called Baedeker targets, they might well have achieved their objective of putting the R.A.F. out of action. He replied that we had wasted a lot of bombs in attacking German ball-bearing plants in the belief that they were the vulnerable point in their armament production. He later admitted in his memoirs, published after his release, that our bomber attacks had almost put an end to German ball-bearing production. On this kind of theme it might be pointed out that, though German fighter production increased enormously towards the end of the war, they were largely put out of action by Allied bombing of their fuel supplies.

The German air attacks during the summer and autumn of 1940 ranged from the north-east coast to the South Wales docks. Many think of the Battle of Britain as taking place over Kent and Sussex, but the Germans had many objectives – shipping, airfields, London, the ports and the industrial north.

Our first batch of enemy crashes came from the attacks on the South Wales docks, followed by the assault on the Channel until well into August. About the middle of August the Germans carried out a heavy raid made up of bombers and fighters from Norway on the Tyne and another on the Yorkshire coast. They obviously thought that all our air defences would be concentrated in the south-east, but the blow had been anticipated by Fighter Command and Dowding's reserve squadrons were already in the north-east. Over Yorkshire and Northumberland the Luftwaffe suffered one of the first of its defeats. This battle in the north gave us a good list of shot-down aircraft and I found myself detached for a time to H.Q. Northern Command at York. I was picking up the pieces with other officers from Morpeth to the mouth of the Humber.

The game book produced quite a number of Ju 88 bombers. Again and again in my notes I find the cause of the crash – fighter action. However, I also have a note to procure the tail swastika of one aircraft for Second Lieutenant Martin of No. 358 Battery at a place called Halsham. As I have mentioned before, we often had to decide if the credit for a shot-down aircraft had to go to a fighter or the A.A. – or both. This was a question which could at times be answered by survivors of German air crews.

To give one example of a crash report, I have some details of a Ju 88 brought down at Ottringham on mud flats near the mouth of the Humber. I mention this if only because of the august audience I had for my activities that day. The aircraft had crashed and burnt out. It was a mass of white ash and one of the dirtiest jobs I have ever done. I put on my overalls and climbed down what was left of the fuselage to look inside the tail. While I was inside, I heard my driver call out, "You'd better come out, sir. The Air Marshal's here!" Now the last thing I ever expected to see on a mud flat at the mouth of the Humber was an air marshal. In any case I had always found it a good idea to keep clear of air marshals. They have a habit of asking uncomfortable questions and possibly wondering if one could not be more profitably employed elsewhere.

I crawled out backwards, covered with mud and white ash, and there before me was an air marshal, an air vice-marshal and an air commodore. I have never seen such a display of scrambled eggs on caps. I saluted briskly and the great man introduced himself. He was Air Marshal Sir William Mitchell, Inspector General of the Royal Air Force. He was most kind, to my surprise, and apologized for interrupting me in my work. He said that he was in the neighbourhood and thought he would come over and have a look at the crash. I gave him my report and told him what I was looking for. He then had a look round the few scattered instruments which had escaped the blaze and asked me in rather a hesitant way if he might have a souvenir. I said with all due respect that in no circumstances could anything be removed from an enemy aircraft. However, if he cared to help himself, I was not looking. There was nothing of vital interest to A.I.1(g). So he got his souvenir and duly departed.

The aircraft was a Junkers Ju 88–A1 bomber from the Wildau plant, shot down on 20th August 1940. Its identification markings were 4D + IS, the I being in black with a white outline. The engines (two) were Jumo 211s. The condition of the aircraft was that it was burnt out and the cause of the crash was fighter action and ground defence. Hence the request from Second Lieutenant Martin of the A.A. Battery. Armament consisted of three machine guns, one in the nose, the others unascertainable but presumably lateral. There were sixteen magazines of ammunition and the aircraft carried four 250 kg bombs, which had been jettisoned. There were no mines or mine carriers. There was no armour plate protection for the crew. There had been a crew of four. Three were prisoners with the Cameron Highlanders and one had since died. There were seven bullet holes in the port engine and eight in the starboard, all aft. Good shooting by the fighter concerned. No samples of petrol or oil could be obtained, as it was burnt out. It carried the usual BZG 2 bombsight. Other instruments, navigational, radio and so on were destroyed. Recommended disposal – junkyard. That was an example of a rather unproductive examination. Nothing new but at least one aircraft less on the Luftwaffe strength.

I mentioned prisoners. There was one curious thing which struck me several times. One would have expected that German airmen stood a fair chance of being lynched by infuriated citizens whose homes they had been bombing half an hour before. I never heard of any cases of survivors being attacked. In fact on more than one occasion, on asking where the prisoners were, I heard that someone was giving them a cup of tea somewhere until the military or the police arrived to take them over.

It was a few days before this crash that the Luftwaffe struck its heaviest blow, throwing in about eighteen hundred aircraft, fighters and bombers, on 15th August in five major attacks. This was the biggest air battle so far and it was fought right across England on a front of over five hundred miles. It ended in a defeat for the Germans. Our squadrons in the south were engaged again and again. What our men lacked in numbers they made up in tenacity. Figures of the relative losses are still argued. We at the Air Ministry were in as good a position as any to know how many enemy aircraft had been shot down, but they were crashes on land. In the fighting round our coasts many aircraft were shot down into the sea. Then again two of our fighters might claim the same aircraft. Two or more observers on land might see the same one crash in the coastal waters. German figures always differed from ours and both sides were naturally inclined to be optimistic. Suffice it to say that German losses were such that Goering had to begin to practise some economy in his strategy.

However, as far as we on the ground were concerned, there were very large numbers of enemy aircraft now dropping from the sky. Every available officer was out all over England, dashing from one crash to another and telephoning reports to harassed duty officers at the Air Ministry throughout the day and night. I spent most of my time in the Scarborough and Bridlington area examining one Ju 88 after another but never getting to the end of my list. In the early months of the war crashes were so few that it was quite a distinction to be selected to go out on a job. We were now overwhelmed and even our WAAF drivers had to help in going through the wreckage. Enemy equipment of all kinds began to accumulate: bombsights, radio sets,

Crash landing by a German trainer aircraft. Photograph found on a careless **POW**.

Air Intelligence officers examining wing section of a Ju 188. Wreckage was often widely scattered and in the most inconvenient places.

Examination of Me 210 twin-seater fighter forced down on the Sangro in the Italian campaign.

Tail section of Ju 188. Air Intelligence officers decide it is a write-off.

machine guns and cannon, bombs, ammunition, navigation instruments, petrol tanks, engines and propellers. R.A.E. Farnborough, the Ordnance Board, H.M.S. *Vernon*, Woolwich, the Ministry of Aircraft Production and many other bodies all required material for examination and test. In fact we later delivered whole bombers and fighters to Farnborough, where they were serviced by our own ground staff and flown by British pilots. Spare parts were often required and had to be supplied from subsequent crashes.

Among the crashes near Bridlington was a Ju 88 which was very badly smashed up. There was very little left of interest in the wreckage, but apparently a fairing with two extra machine guns firing aft had been jettisoned before the crash and was found close by almost intact. We had not seen this additional armament before. This was the kind of information which was vital to our fighters. Previously the Ju 88 had forward and lateral firing guns. Now our pilots would have to be prepared for a burst when they were attacking from the rear. The Ju 88 was a very fine aircraft and by the standards of those days very fast. With the nose down it could give a fighter a very good run for its money. I had another Ju 88 which had exploded on impact over a very wide area, yet one unexploded bomb was found almost buried under some of the debris. Fortunately the R.E.s had the job of dealing with that. I find in my notes – "Crew, presumably four to judge by miscellaneous human remains." This was unusual, as quite a number of crews had managed to bale out in the battles over Yorkshire.

I also had a note at that time to collect more instruments and other equipment for our museum, now located at Ryder Street. These were needed for the instruction of more and more new officers coming in to deal with the ever growing number of aircraft brought down and for demonstration to visitors from our own and other services. We were joined by two regular officers who really did understand what went on inside the various wireless and navigational instruments we collected. They actually made them work, to the amazement of those of us to whom this new science of radar and electronics was a complete mystery.

This branch of intelligence became of vital importance when the Germans developed an accurate system of bombing by means of a radio beam – or rather two beams, which could pinpoint a target whatever the weather. Accurate to within a matter of a few hundred yards, it would save them much time and trouble in training crews in navigation.

The story began with a shot-down German bomber fitted with an apparatus, which was found to be rather more complicated than that needed for its normal homing and night-landing on the Lorenz beam with which we were familiar. This discovery, together with information from other sources, suggested to our experts that the Germans were planning a system of navigating and bombing on a beam system. Papers recovered from other shot-down aircraft and some hints gathered in the course of an interrogation of a captured bomber pilot associated this theory with the code-name "Knickebein" which had been engaging our attention. This discovery and its implications were of such importance that Dr R.V. Jones, of Scientific Intelligence at the Air Ministry, was summoned to the Cabinet Room to explain how it was likely to work to the Prime Minister himself. Dr Jones, whom I came to know at the end of the war in another branch of our intelligence services, was then a young man who had studied under Professor Lindemann, later Lord Cherwell, at Oxford. He could not have been more surprised to find himself pushed into the limelight of a meeting with the Prime Minister attended by senior R.A.F. officers and distinguished men of science. What he had to say convinced his audience that "Knickebein" was a serious menace and could cause untold damage to our cities unless counter-measures could be quickly devised and put into operation.

Once the system was known and understood, it was a straight-forward job for our "boffins" and R.A.F. specialists in blind flying to work out a way of nullifying the German efforts. But it was the quick thinking and interpretation of intelligence by men like Dr Jones which enabled us to get on with the solution of the problem in good time.

The detection of "Knickebein" in operation and the measures taken to counter that and other German devices to place their bombers in all weathers exactly over their targets not only saved many an objective from destruction but gave us warning of attacks and a chance of bringing our night-fighters and A.A. defences into action at the right time and in the right place. Without doubt the Germans underestimated the work of our Intelligence in this field and they certainly wasted many hundreds of tons of bombs in open country before they realized that we were disrupting their plans.

XIV

In due course the Germans did realize that we were distorting half of their "Knickebein" beam and deflecting the bomber pilot from his course, so they introduced another system known as the "X-Gerät" or "X apparatus". This was a cross-beam system and in fact was used in the attack on Coventry. This too was duly jammed and turned to our advantage, after which the "Y-Gerät" or "Y apparatus" appeared. It was a single beam along which the bomber travelled a set distance before releasing his bomb load.

I have mentioned these different types of beam bombing very briefly and given what I hope is a simple explanation, but I should like to stress that the research and detective work in mastering the German systems and the putting into action of counter-measures were anything but brief and simple. I have also limited my account of this, which was only one aspect of the high-frequency war – to borrow the Prime Minister's phrase – because I am not technically qualified to deal in detail with such a subject. Indeed it would be impertinent of me to comment on the work of scientists of the calibre of Dr Jones. I have made mention of the "Knickebein" story merely to show how important it was to examine each and every part of the equipment of an enemy aircraft for any novelty or modification, which could lead far greater experts in intelligence, research and development to valuable discoveries of this kind.

Even before the appearance of "Knickebein", we had had some success in leading German aircraft astray by picking up their signals on ordinary directional wireless, amplifying them and re-transmitting them from parts of England. I had to examine one German bomber, which was returning from an attack on South Wales and was apparently tricked into landing in South Devon. One of the crew said that they had mistaken the Bristol Channel for the English Channel. This aircraft had taken off from Holland and was to have returned to a French airfield on completion of the bombing mission. The crew had stocked up on Dutch chocolate and various groceries against their landing in Paris where supplies were possibly not so plentiful. I was thus able to return from my mission to Honiton with enough chocolate to last my children for some time.

One of the bullet-proof petrol tanks on this aircraft had burst open. This particular type of tank developed by the Germans consisted principally of three layers of rubber forming a kind of sandwich. There were two layers of indurated rubber, between which was one layer of non-indurated rubber. A bullet piercing this sandwich would release enough petrol to act on the non-indurated rubber and form a temporary seal. These self-sealing tanks, as they were called, also had two or three other coverings, the purpose of which was to soften the impact of the bullet. One of these coverings was a whole cowhide. This was my other trophy from the Devon crash. It was made into a very stout and practical hold-all for my journeys.

Towards the end of August the Luftwaffe threw in aircraft at the rate of over a thousand a day in an attempt to break the power of the R.A.F. in preparation for the invasion. On 16th August no less than 1,720, most of them fighters, attacked southern England. As the month went on, Sussex, Kent, Essex and London were the main objectives. Raids on the north-east fell off, so I left my comfortable quarters at the Royal Station Hotel in York and returned to London. There were far too many enemy crashed aircraft for the Maintenance Units to pick up. Practically all our officers were concentrated in the south-east, rushing from one aircraft to another as they were shot down. There were Dornier 17s, Junkers 88s, Heinkel 111s and Messerschmitt 109s and 110s. It was not only German aircraft which were strewn all over the countryside. Our fighters were facing a determined and redoubtable enemy, many of them fine airmen and well equipped. Our own losses were getting dangerously high, not only in the defence of our country but in the attacks which we were making on German invasion concentrations and other objectives on the Continent. We were losing many of our best men fast and others were picked up frightfully burned and mutilated.

My own crashes ranged from a Messerschmitt 109 in a back street in Plumstead to a number of Messerschmitt 110s in the Enfield and Ponder's End area. They were mainly burnt out, cause of crash – fighter action. There were many crashes in the London area itself. One Dornier bomber landed on Victoria Station in September. Every time we drove out of London towards the south or south-east we had to take a different route. Every day more streets were blocked by crashes, air raid damage, broken water mains or bomb craters.

After a spell in the London area, I went down to Sussex. Here there were more Me 110s — at Wisborough Green, Washington, Black Patch Hill and other peaceful little places which had suddenly become a battlefield. Some of the aircraft we examined now bore records on the tail fin of victories over French and British aircraft. There were so many aircraft to deal with that guards were often inadequate and the souvenir hunters had a wonderful time. Equipment sometimes had to be salvaged from the local pub and one of our own officers was said to have hidden a complete Messerschmitt 109 in a garage in one of the south coast towns for disposal after the war!

Attacks on the Thames estuary brought us another crop of crashes in Essex. I had nothing but Me 110s again and they were almost all completely destroyed by fighter action. I had one at Upminster, two at Laindon and one at Billericay on the same day. To anyone who experienced the Zeppelin raids of the first war, the names of Billericay and Cuffley near Potter's Bar stand out. They were the sites of two Zeppelin crashes. I remember as a boy seeing the sky to the north of London lit up as a blazing Zeppelin fell at Cuffley. A Zeppelin crash was a fearful and dramatic spectacle. There was no escape by parachute in those days and the enormous volume of gas burned fiercely. They were over 700 feet long and carried a crew of about twenty. When I was examining the Me 110 at Billericay, a retired policeman helping to guard the wreckage told me that he had been one of the first on the scene of the crash of Zeppelin L.32 there in 1916. A gigantic mass of aluminium framework extended over several large fields. Part of the wreck was over a hundred feet high. His first impression was the appalling smell of the burnt bodies. It must have taken weeks to clear up a crash in those days. Mine produced very little; a partly buried DB 601 engine plus a parachute and a Mae West of a new type which I collected from Billericay Police Station. Of the crew of two, a lieutenant was captured. The gunner was wounded and died later.

As time went on, we gathered up vast quantities of German equipment and distributed it to various government departments as well as to firms manufacturing similar material. We found rubber dinghies for fighters and bombers as well as inflatable floats to keep bombers from sinking in the sea until the crew had got out. We found throat microphones on flying helmets and electrically heated gloves and fuel injection in the German engines. So far materials, design and workmanship were first-class but we were always looking for "Ersatz" products which might betray a weakness in the German war economy. The word "Ersatz" came to be used disparagingly over here but the German expression, pronounced incidentally with the accent on the second syllable, simply means compensation, replacement or substitute. Some substitute materials were better than the original ones. Though the Germans were forced to certain shifts later in the war, the quality of their equipment remained high.

Though I was relieved that we did not have to deal with unexploded bombs, we did have to handle quite a lot of lethal devices. Apart from guns and ammunition which we collected from aircraft, there were the explosive charges I have mentioned for destroying aircraft in the event of a forced landing. Until the Germans had such charges built in, they sometimes carried a couple of hand grenades. Then there were Very pistols, very much in demand as souvenirs, Lueger, Mauser and Walther automatic pistols and even Schmeisser and Walther submachine guns.

The Germans are born tourists. They often carried their own cameras on board. We acquired a whole range of different makes, sometimes containing films taken on the other side, which we developed and on occasion found to be of considerable intelligence value.

A number of amusing security posters were produced during the war for the 2nd Tactical Air Force by an artist called Masquelier of the Lorraine Squadron. One showed a young airman about to enter a bordello turning out his pockets under the red light. The caption reads – Do not forget to empty your pockets before leaving on ops! It was a strict rule with us but we found the Germans were very careless, as in the case of the complete handbook of the Ju 88, which was a wonderful find for a technical intelligence department. Another Masquelier poster depicted a girl showing rather more leg than usual with the warning – She knows what you're after and she's after what you know!

Fortunately for me, we had very few German speakers on our staff. The German scholars were likely to be snapped up by our interrogation unit, A.I.1(k). Thus I was given a number of interesting jobs as well as some very sticky chores in translating. One experience which I was glad not to have missed was a short spell with Codes and

Cyphers at Bletchley. This institution was shrouded in mystery till some time after the war. Suffice it to say that I have seldom had such an interesting job in my life. We lived cut off from the world outside by maximum security measures among an amazing collection of very gifted people. In Hut 3 I worked with a number of distinguished German scholars, my own contribution being that I knew what the parts of an aircraft were called in German and I had some idea of the organization of the Luftwaffe. Whatever a professor of German may know about the *Nibelungenlied* or Goethe's Conversations with Eckermann, he is unlikely to have the faintest idea what a reduction gear or a retractable undercarriage are in German. Hence I found myself consulted by giants in the world of philology, whose shoes I was not worthy to unlace.

Yet a knowledge of the old German legends could also be useful at times. In the high-frequency war it was noticed that the Germans gave names from the operas of the Ring to certain types of apparatus. Now the Germans are a very methodical and consistent people in some things and the names they gave to these items of equipment furnished us with a clue to their function – provided that someone was on hand who was familiar with the *Nibelungenlied*. Thus it was clear that their "Wotan-Gerät" worked with a single beam and that the "Freya-Gerät" was ancillary, Wotan being one-eyed and Freya being the handmaid of the Gods.

The story of the work done in Hut 3 at Bletchley Park has been recounted in Group Captain F.W. Winterbotham's book *The Ultra Secret*. God knows we started the war with almost everything against us but we did have the incredible good fortune to acquire the reputedly unbreakable German machine cyphers at the very beginning. Happily it never occurred to the Germans that we could break the Enigma Cypher. We were thus able to supply our commanders in the field and, later, our American allies with intelligence of the enemy's plans, order of battle, deficiencies, day-to-day situation and even the Fuehrer's exhortations and reproaches to *his* commanders throughout the war. By another stroke of luck for us, the Germans had sold a version of the Enigma machine to the Japanese. They adapted it and used it so that we and the Americans had a coverage of the operations in the Pacific into the bargain. When I was in Hut 3, much of our Ultra, as this form of intelligence was called, was concentrated on the war in North Africa. My own impression at that time and later was that Ultra went a long way towards getting the Germans out of that theatre of war. As time went on, the weaknesses of the enemy supply lines across the Mediterranean became more and more apparent. We almost had a Bradshaw of naval and air traffic and we made good use of it. The greatest credit must of course go to the code-breakers, the group of mathematicians and cryptographers at Bletchley, with whose work I had nothing to do. They supplied the real goods to us.

The job in Hut 3 was interpretation, evaluation, prompt distribution of the intelligence while it could still be of practical use and, above all, protection of the source. The enemy could not be allowed to guess that any success on the part of our commanders might be due to a fore-knowledge gained from radio intercepts. Thus credible alternative sources had to be invented and the real source protected at all costs. There was always the risk that commanders in the field might act rashly with the bonus of the enemy's situation and intentions in their hands. British and American leaders reacted in different ways, varying with their personalities, but the secret was kept till the end. Group Captain Winterbotham comments on the attitudes adopted by various commanders and refers to those with orthodox methods of fighting an enemy. They seemed to think that it was not quite right to know beforehand what the enemy was going to do. This curious mentality recalls the view held by some soldiers in the 1914–18 war that it was not sporting to use a periscope in the trenches. Fortunately the practical view prevailed and full advantage was taken of the Ultra delivered from Bletchley.

Among the most accomplished natural linguists in Hut 3 one of the outstanding characters was Group Captain Harry Humphreys. I had already met him at Arras when I remarked on his fluency in French. When I was first introduced into the mysteries of Bletchley Park I was picked up at a rendezvous in London by a chauffeur, who was armed with a revolver and police truncheon, and driven northwards, quite unaware of my destination. We arrived late at night in total darkness. After passing two barriers, I was taken to a small hut, lit by a single light bulb, and told to sit at a bare table. An officer placed a paper in front of me and I saw that it contained an extract from the Official Secrets Act. I said I had been through all this before, but I was told not only to sign it but to read if carefully first. My initiation completed, I was led through the darkness to the entrance of one of a number of long huts. When the second black-out door was opened with a blaze of light, I found I was among many friends including

Harry Humphreys, this time as fluent in German as he was in French.

Hut 3 was full of "characters", including one titled lady who, on hearing that a poor family had been evicted from their cottage, suggested in a Marie-Antoinette voice that they could go to a hotel. There were many officers like myself who had travelled widely in Europe and been recruited for intelligence work, finally landing up in the innermost sanctuary of Bletchley Park. Almost all of us were amateurs in uniform. In fact I cannot remember any regular R.A.F. officers. I had one colleague in my line of technical and scientific intelligence, an elderly flight lieutenant called De Haan. Despite his name, he was the Italian expert. For many years he had represented a well-known British firm of armament manufacturers, which had supplied torpedoes to the Italian Navy. His knowledge of Italian and his technical background helped out when we had any problems arising out of German and Italian co-operation in the battle of the Mediterranean.

In Hut 3 there were civilians, male and female, as well as Army and R.A.F. officers. Among them were university dons who kept records and built up pictures on various subjects, producing reports which we had to plough through in addition to the never-ending stream of tapes coming from the cryptographers. A prominent figure was Professor Frederick ("Bimbo") Norman, of the University of London and head of the department of German at King's College. He had the distinction of possessing a cubby-hole of his own while we sat at tables in the main hut. He would occasionally emerge with a red face demanding "What rubbish is this?" I was terrified of him. Well might I be! A veteran of the Ruhleben internment camp of the First World War, he had afterwards studied at University College, London, under some very distinguished philologists. Among his specialities was Medieval German, in which he was at one time reader at King's College and University College. He had assisted the B.B.C. at the beginning of the war with German broadcasting and the selection of German personnel, some of whom I was to meet later when I began broadcasting to the Luftwaffe. I came in contact with him when he came out to Germany as an honorary Wing Commander to take part in the reconstruction of the German universities. I gathered that one of his tasks was the rescue of "Minerva", the international directory of learned bodies, which was published in Germany. He stayed with me at times in my house in Bad Salzuflen. By then I had lost my fear of him and we became friends. He would entertain us after dinner with recitations from Chaucer in his version of the pronunciation of the fourteenth century. He well deserved his nickname of "Bimbo", the Italian word for a child, for, despite his occasional ferocity and unwillingness to suffer fools gladly, he had a sense of schoolboy fun and never lost the youthful enthusiasm which he so ably transmitted. That is the essence of good teaching and he was an admirable teacher. He held many important posts and gained many distinctions before he died in 1968.

With a gathering of stars employed in a cloistered atmosphere such as we had at Bletchley, life was remarkably stimulating. At the long lunch or dinner tables one might find oneself sitting next or opposite to some well-known writer, scientist, mathematician, industrialist or social celebrity. With such a job in hand all manner of talent had been recruited. Shop was out as a subject of conversation so the talk was on every other subject, often above my head but never dull. I sat like Saul at the feet of so many Gamaliels and just listened.

Those of us who were exiled to such exclusive institutions as Bletchley Park or the Riding School at Woburn Abbey, which I also had occasion to visit, were said to be "in the country". Even today, when I meet retired veterans of those branches of intelligence, now living in Kent and Sussex near my own home, the expression "in the country" serves as an immediate introduction and password.

Inside Hut 3 it was always daytime as in a submarine. On a night watch I often had my dinner at 2 or 3 o'clock in the morning. By 6 a.m. I was drinking unsweetened black coffee in large mugs over an incomprehensible tape, puzzling out what the sender was up to, or trying to work out the meaning of yet another German expression or abbreviation which had never been found in any dictionary but had come into use since the beginning of the war.

For me it was a unique experience to have been "on the inside" of this invaluable operation for a brief period and indeed I took it as a compliment, for absolute secrecy had to be observed by every individual working behind the wire at Bletchley. Every landlady in that town, in Leighton Buzzard and other localities where we lodged and every pub gossip was agog to know what went on there. Not a word leaked out throughout the whole war, though I did hear that there had been an alarm when one of those employed inside had gone into a pub with a short length of tape stuck to the sole of his shoe. A colleague fortunately spotted it and it was quickly removed. It might have given someone a hint of what was going on. I have noticed that women are much more security conscious than men. Men may be tempted to boast to their girl friends or hint at their employment on some mysterious project while women have other means to attract the interest of the opposite sex.

The peak point of the Battle of Britain was 15th September, on which date a record number of enemy aircraft losses was announced. As we knew at the time, since we had details of all crashes, the figure was considerably exaggerated. It was not corrected till long after, but it did public morale a lot of good at that stage of the war. Then we passed the point where Operation "Sealion" was called off. The imminent danger of invasion was over and the first Battle of Britain had been won. But air attacks went on and we had plenty of crashes from the Tyne to Cornwall.

While the Battle of Britain was on, we still had many headaches in other parts of the world. Enemy aircraft were being shot down in North Africa. These included Italian aircraft though we did not take these very seriously. There were no trained officers out there or indeed anyone who had the time to make detailed reports, so we had to train officers to go out to Cairo. They followed the fortunes of that war to and fro along the North African coast and some of them eventually went ashore with the first wave of the Italian landings, carrying on up into Europe until some who had started in Cairo landed up in Klagenfurt in Austria. Other officers were sent out to India where they specialized in Japanese aircraft. One unfortunate A.I.1(g) officer got himself a job on Arctic convoys. With the Luftwaffe operating from northern Norway, we had to have someone to identify aircraft and possibly deal with intercepted signals. He was a City stockbroker in civil life, a most unlikely choice for such a chore. Happily he survived.

My museum of German equipment grew and its fame spread. Groups of all kinds of people from the various services used to visit us for study and lectures. We also had officers working there who made a speciality of German aircraft performances. They worked out, for the benefit of our fighters, the capabilities of the various types of German aircraft with much brandishing of slide-rules. Squadron Leader Michael Golovine of Rolls Royce and later of Hawker Siddeley was our chief expert in this field.

In due course we accumulated a collection of complete German aircraft at Farnborough. Force-landed or slightly damaged aircraft were repaired and flown on tests against our own aircraft. I once had to examine a Ju 88, which force-landed through engine trouble on

Oakington Aerodrome near Cambridge. It was a belly landing with little damage beyond buckling the airscrew blades of one engine. With cranes we got it up on its undercarriage, towed it into a hangar and delivered it to Farnborough where I eventually saw it fly. We had to train R.A.F. personnel to service these aircraft and had to make our own metric gauge tools for this purpose. After I left the unit which had become A.I.2(g), I heard that a He 111, carrying some of our ground crew, had had to take violent evasive action while being flown with a captured Me 110. It stalled while coming in to land and crashed, killing all on board.

One day in May 1941 we received among the daily crash advices a report of a Me 110 down at such and such a map reference in Scotland — "pilot believed to be Rudolf Hess". I took over from the Night Duty Officer the logbook in which all telephone messages were recorded. At first we treated the Hess story as a joke. It so happened that we had a newly joined junior officer, who used to receive a lot of private telephone calls. They were usually from people with very high-sounding names and titles. All calls had to be logged and these entries became a standing joke. Message for Pilot Officer so and so. Air Marshal this or that phoned. Princess Anonyma rang and so on. Thus we were inclined to put the Hess message in this category. Anyway, we duly instructed our local man at Carluke to proceed to the crash for the routine examination, as he was nearest to it. We were rather intrigued, as that part of Scotland was beyond the range of the Me 110. I think it was afterwards established that it was fitted with an extra fuel tank.

Then all hell broke loose. It *was* Hess. Within a short time Sir Ivone Kirkpatrick, formerly our Counsellor in Berlin, was on his way to identify him and the Fuehrer had a nice political headache to handle. The rest of the story is too well known to be repeated here. I saw Hess at Nuremberg and in my opinion he was and is mentally unbalanced. However, at the time of writing this, I see no purpose in running a large prison to keep this now harmless and pitiful old man locked up.

Our enemy crash group had grown into a large and very important branch of Intelligence, staffed by a number of well-qualified and experienced officers who knew most of the answers about the Luftwaffe and its equipment. Some had moved to an underground fortress three floors down in Monck Street, Westminster. It was built on a circular site where a gasometer had been destroyed. Here we dwelt like moles, rarely coming up for air unless we were out on a crash job. There were several branches of Air Intelligence in this dungeon and conditions were such that we all had to have sun-ray treatment every day. We had to strip down to a pair of dark goggles when half a dozen of us at a time, air commodores to dog's-bodies, sat round the lamp for the set period.

Down in the depths we heard nothing of raids or alarms or rain or sunshine. It was quite a shock to come up from the peaceful life underground to find an air raid on. I once caught a blacked-out bus creeping along Victoria Street in a heavy raid. I felt very frightened and I could not help marvelling at the courage of the driver and the conductor. All I wanted to do was to crawl underground again. When I got to Trafalgar Square, I stood talking to a policeman standing at the top of the stairs leading down to the Tube. These entrances had been covered over with concrete slabs for protection. The noise overhead was deafening. "You'd better get inside, sir," said the policeman. I did. It was just in time as a large piece of hot metal came down with a crack where I had been standing.

One day I left Monck Street at about five o'clock to walk up to Trafalgar Square past the Abbey. On an impulse I went in. I had not been in the Abbey for years. I was surprised to find it packed to the door. Wondering what was going to happen, I found a seat on a tomb. Then, as if they had been waiting for my arrival, the performance began. It was the *Messiah* with Isobel Bailey singing. That this could happen in the midst of the war with a fair chance of a bomb in the vicinity seemed a miracle. Forgetting that I was on my way home, I stayed to the end. It was a moving and unforgettable experience. Yet I had a similar one in the occupation of Germany after the war. In the desolation and near starvation of immediate post-war Germany I went into a little church in Westphalia to find it full of people wrapped against the cold, listening to a recital of the music of Bach and Buxtehude. I suppose there is some hope for the human race.

XV

Renowned as the British are for their amateur approach to most subjects, even those of war and self-preservation, I doubt very much if the Germans would have believed that one comparatively junior regular officer and a few untrained civilians in uniform sitting in an infants' school in Harrow Weald in 1939 constituted the main centre of information on the aircraft of the Luftwaffe. It is true that another department of the Air Ministry was concerned with the organization of the Luftwaffe, its order of battle, locations and so on, but we knew really little about its aircraft and equipment at the beginning of the war. For some months the only enemy aircraft we had to work on was the Heinkel 111 brought down near Dalkeith in Scotland in 1939.

Although the German and Italian air forces had been trying out their aircraft in the Spanish Civil War, it does not seem to have occurred to many of us that, within a few years, some of those aircraft would be attacking our troops in France and dropping bombs on London. The experience gained in Spain in the thirties was a very important part of the build-up between the wars of that highly efficient Luftwaffe, which was to win lightning victories for the German forces in the first two or three years of the war and which came very near to destroying us all.

Despite the terms of the Treaty of Versailles, the Germans lost no time in making preparations for a renascent flying corps. As early as May 1920, General von Seeckt in an order of the day disbanding the air branch of the German armed forces had expressed the hope of an eventual resurgence. Not much later, training began under various forms of camouflage of those who would in due course form the framework of the Luftwaffe, just as the minimal army permitted by the Treaty would become the N.C.O.s of the hundreds of divisions, which would control Europe from the Arctic to the Black Sea. Some of the clandestine training took place in Russia, beginning in 1925 after the Treaty of Rapallo under the guise of Russo-German collaboration in aeronautics. The first training aircraft were procured and smuggled into Russia from the Dutch firm of Fokker. The Russian school was at first equipped with Fokker D XIII fighter aircraft. Little did the Dutch know at that time that the Luftwaffe they were helping to train would one day bomb Rotterdam flat. Meanwhile Ernst Heinkel was playing hide-and-seek with the Allied Control Commission developing aircraft destined for co-operation with the German army. A few of these were used at the training centre at Lipezk in Russia. By the time Germany abandoned the training of future pilots in Russia, early types of Heinkel, Arado, Junkers and Dornier aircraft had been tested out there.

On Hitler's seizure of power, Germany was confident enough to abandon the Russian link and come out into the open. Our government was not strong enough to call the bluff either then or in 1936, when Germany re-armed the Rhineland. Some pilots had been trained for a time in Italian flying schools, but the time had come in 1935 when Hitler could issue a decree making the Reichsluftwaffe into an independent branch of the armed forces. Germany had an air force and the defeat of 1918 could be forgotten. Squadrons were given heroic titles and Goering began a morale-boosting campaign. Names such as those of Immelmann, Richthofen and Boelke were applied to squadrons and the notorious Condor Legion came into being. The outstanding achievement of that Air Force unit was the obliteration of Guernica, a foretaste of the wrath that was to come if we had only recognized it. Somehow the full title of Reichsluftwaffe never caught on and the German Air Force came to be known simply as the Luftwaffe.

This is not the place for a history of the German Air Force. We are concerned here with what our Air Staff knew about this new and efficient arm of the German forces in 1939. In the thirties there had of course been the usual exchange visits of top brass of the Royal Air Force and the Luftwaffe and some of our more junior officers, like my former colleague in France, had been on courses in Germany. One report came back that the Luftwaffe had accurate models of all our aircraft, but we certainly had none of theirs. When it was suggested that we might do something about it, it was stated that there was not even a draughtsman at the Air Ministry to make drawings of German aircraft, not to speak of models. There was no establishment for a draughtsman. Therefore there was no draughtsman. However, a

Me 110 with British markings flown by RAFwaffe flying circus.

Ju 88 at the RAFwaffe air base at Collyweston.

The other Germany. A decorated house in Bad Salzuflen, to which Pastor Johan Loofher brought his bride, Anna Resen, in 1621.

draughtsman could be introduced under the disguise of a map-maker, but he would have to take a mapping course! It was almost as if we and not the Germans were the ones operating clandestinely. They had long camouflaged all their activities in building up the Luftwaffe and that was understandable. Yet we were unable to justify the employment of a draughtsman to make drawings of German aircraft. Meanwhile our own Royal Air Force apparently had little idea what German aircraft looked like unless they read the international aero-nautical press. When I began among the founding members of A.I.1(g), our files were largely drawn from illustrations from *Flight* and *The Aeroplane* on our side and heroic pictures from German and Italian magazines. All manner of official "war artists" were appointed to record the progress of the war for posterity but few, if any, would have been capable of producing an accurate and operationally useful diagram of any aircraft.

Eventually, three very competent artists were added to the establishment as "draughtsmen". A high degree of skill was required and we were very fortunate in being able to recruit Kerry Lee, Hubert Redmill and Peter Endsleigh Castle. Kerry Lee, well known for his amusing pictorial maps of London, Oxford, Cambridge and other cities, had studied in Paris in his youth. He was a most versatile and gifted artist, able to turn his hand to the technical problems we gave him and produce the most accurate drawings and diagrams while entertaining us in his spare time with delightfully satirical comments in line and wash on the follies of the human race.

Hubert Redmill had trained as a commercial artist. He was particularly useful to us as he did know something about flying, having obtained his pilot's "A" licence just before the war. He had volunteered for ferry work but had failed on account of his limited number of flying hours – happily for us, as his work was of a very high standard both technically and artistically. Finally we had Peter Endsleigh Castle, still well known for his aircraft diagrams and as an illustrator in many fields. He had been invited before the war into A.I.1(a), when it was the nucleus of Air Intelligence, as an expert on aircraft recognition. It was he who had to be disguised as a map-maker to get in at all!

All three were able to combine accuracy and observation in the well-known posters they produced of the aircraft and equipment of the Luftwaffe, an exact knowledge of which was vital to the R.A.F., A.A., Army, Navy, Observer Corps, A.R.P., Home Guard and anyone else who had to be familiar not only with the appearance but with the performance of the enemy's aircraft.

For the first two years of the war and as attacks on Britain increased we concentrated on the aircraft already mentioned, the three principal German bomber types and the two Messerschmitt fighters. Those who served in the war will remember these posters and recognition diagrams distributed throughout the country. It seems hardly credible that these were the work of the three underpaid artists of A.I.2(g), working not in a properly equipped studio such as any good advertising agency would consider absolutely necessary but in a class-room of an elementary school. Attempts to get them commissioned in the R.A.F. to ensure a living wage for them met with the usual establishment excuses. As artists in peacetime they could have commanded worthwhile salaries and in wartime they would have been very well paid as draughtsmen in aircraft factories. However, they stayed on and produced, from all manner of sources, a collection of drawings and diagrams which contributed very considerably to our war effort and which are still an accurate record of the development of the equipment of the Luftwaffe. This accuracy was amply confirmed when our intelligence officers were able to check their work on the spot after the war in Germany.

As in our own Air Force, the aircraft of the Luftwaffe were developed and improved as the war progressed. Our diagrams had to be kept up to date as performances changed, modifications were introduced and as armament, protective armour and arcs of fire varied. The R.A.F. Interrogation Officers kept us supplied with vital information, rumours and even day-to-day changes in nomenclature. I kept a record of new technical expressions, abbreviations or slang. When the War Office in 1943 had their *Vocabulary of German Military Terms and Abbreviations* published by H.M. Stationery Office, I was able to contribute many of the air terms.

Although I was to leave A.I.2(g) in the summer of 1942, I kept in touch with the ever-growing army of intelligence officers engaged in the examination and evaluation of enemy aircraft. They had long outgrown the infants' school and the office of the Charity Commissioners and were working in a large Victorian country house at Harrow Weald. It was by virtue of our long residence at Harrow Weald that we were made honorary members of Fighter Command Mess at Bentley Priory, not far from the "The Manor", our new home.

America and Russia were now in the war and material and

information streamed in from all the battle fronts. American officers came to be trained at "The Manor" and our own officers were co-operating with American air bases in Britain.

The big news just as I was leaving was the advent of Professor Kurt Tank's Focke-Wulf Fw 190. When he was interrogated in 1945, he paid Peter Endsleigh Castle the compliment of signing a photocopy of his A.I.2(g) cutaway drawing of the Fw 190D–9, now in the Imperial War Museum.

Like my almost intact Ju 88, which landed at Oakington, our first Focke-Wulf fighter was a lucky break for us. Although I had no hand in this investigation, the circumstances are worth recording. On the evening of 23rd June 1942, Oberleutnant Arnim Faber, the adjutant of III/JG 2 (fighter unit), landed his Fw 190A–3 at R.A.F. Pembrey. Although his Staffel (unit of nine aircraft) had been in combat with Spitfires of the Exeter-based Polish Wing returning from a strike on Morlaix airfield, Faber's aircraft was undamaged, so his reason for landing was obscure. It is possible that he mistook the Bristol Channel for the English Channel and imagined he was landing on a Luftwaffe airfield in northern France. This would not have been the first time a German pilot had made that mistake. This theory is borne out by the series of victory rolls he performed before touching down.

As in the case of the Ju 88, this perfect specimen of the Fw 190 was rushed off to Farnborough for complete investigation and flight performance trials by specially qualified R.A.F. test pilots. Experts from the aircraft industry were also called in and their findings influenced British thinking in fighter design for the future, an example of this being the Hawker Tempest. About a year later a Fw 190A–4 landed intact at R.A.F. West Malling after taking part in night intruder operations. This one was finished overall in a matt-black temporary paint. These and many other intact or easily repairable German aircraft were in due course supplied to a R.A.F. "Flying Circus" of enemy aircraft, known as Flight 1426 or the RAFwaffe, based at Collyweston, a satellite airfield to the R.A.F. bomber base at Wittering. This very specialized unit toured British and American air stations for tactical trials with the aircrews there for evaluation of combat characteristics. The German aircraft of course carried British markings.

Intelligence covers a multitude of curious activities, as any student of James Bond's adventures will admit. However, it is not always the spectacular feats which change the course of history. As I learned in my brief sojourn at Bletchley, infinite patience in a sedentary job can sometimes produce sensational results. Observation, expert knowledge, logical thinking and prompt action in a hut in the Buckinghamshire countryside must have influenced some very important events in the North African campaign. I can claim no such achievement, but at one stage in the war we owed much to the patience and observation of a young WAAF officer working at the Central Interpretation Unit at Medmenham. Constance Babington Smith, who had been employed before the war as an aeronautical journalist, was engaged on the interpretation of aerial photographs.

Europe is a very large place to cover from the air and the task becomes even more difficult when the area you are photographing is occupied by the enemy. They are concerned not only with covering up what you want to photograph but with preventing your return. We had had all manner of reports from before the war about long-range rockets and there was much talk of pilotless aircraft, until a chance photographic cover of Peenemünde showed some very long objects with fins attached to them. The Air Ministry and the War Office each had their own ideas on what the secret weapon was and how it would be used. However, the whole story has been told by Basil Collier in *The Battle of the V-Weapons*. All we are concerned with here is that in November 1943 Section Officer Babington Smith was puzzling over photographs of Peenemünde taken in June of that year and she was the first of us to see a flying bomb, doodlebug or V.1. Here at last was the pilotless aircraft we had been whispering about and in due course A.I.2(g) had the job of picking up the pieces. Peter Endsleigh Castle did the drawing once we found out exactly what it looked like and how it worked. You can see a copy with one of the original V.1.s in the Science Museum in London. There was a popular idea current at the time that Hitler had spoken of a "Secret Weapon", but as far as I know he never used such an expression. What he said was, "Wir haben eine Waffe gegen die es keine Verteidigung gibt!" (We have a weapon against which there is no defence.) He was no doubt referring to the V.2, against which there *was* no defence then unless you destroyed it at its launching point. The V.1 could be shot down by fighters and A.A. guns. A doodlebug with a fighter in pursuit could be quite a sporting event unless it was heading for a built-up area.

On retrospect I am amazed at the calm way people took what was to build up to a considerable bombardment of south-east England. They would hear the thing coming, wait till the propulsion unit cut

out, take cover or, if indoors, simply duck, listen for the explosion —
hopefully not too close — and then go on doing what they were doing
before.

Throughout the V.1 and V.2 periods A.I.2(g) continued their work
on an increasing number of enemy aircraft types up to the end of the
war. After the Fw 190s, there were the Ju 188s, the Dornier Do 215
and Do 217, the Messerschmitt Me 210 and Me 410, Heinkel He 177s
and, as we moved into the jet age, Me 163s and Me 262s. By then a
very large number of pieces had been picked up since we held our first
amateur inquest on the Heinkel 111 in Scotland. There were A.I.2(g)
officers in every theatre of war, a long way from Hibbert Road School
or the fleshpots of Fighter Command Mess. One young officer,
weighted with a piece of railway line, dived into the Mediterranean to
examine one enemy aircraft. We had no properly equipped frogmen in
those days.

Some officers continued their investigations in Germany and the
former occupied territories, filling in the gaps in our knowledge of the
German aircraft industry and its products. Establishments were set up
to sift and digest the enormous quantities of captured documents.
From seeing through a glass darkly during the war we were now face
to face with the enemy and all his deeds and plans for our destruction.

The extensive junkyards of enemy aircraft are now no more.
However, even today there are still pieces to be picked up in remote
spots. Only two years ago farmers were digging out part of the wreck
of a German aircraft buried deep on the edge of the Romney Marsh.
Many German aircraft must lie in the waters round our shores and
even in the reaches of the Thames. Just as we have dredged the bronze
heads of Roman emperors out of London's river, so some future
archaeologist may one day fish up the engines of a Heinkel 111 and
wonder what this primitive mechanism was used for.

PART III

Speaking to the Enemy

"Hier ist England!"

XVI

It must have been some time in 1942 that a decision was taken at a high level to organize a daily propaganda broadcast from the Royal Air Force to the Luftwaffe. Similar programmes would be directed by the Royal Navy to the Kriegsmarine and by the Army to the Wehrmacht. These transmissions would be part of the B.B.C. European Service, which was already broadcasting propaganda in dozens of different languages. This took the form of factual news programmes to Germany and the peoples of the occupied countries. Apart from presenting the news truthfully they encouraged those peoples in the hope of final liberation. At the same time they were designed to undermine and destroy the morale of the enemy.

Though it was forbidden under dire penalties for Germans and the occupied peoples to listen to our propaganda, it was realized everywhere, even in Germany, that there are two kinds of propaganda; the totalitarian with lies and distortions where necessary to appeal to mass emotions, and the democratic which pre-supposes a free mind and which does not fear to speak the truth. The mere fact that a thing is forbidden, together with the sheer impossibility of having a policeman standing behind every radio set ensured us a good listenership.

There is no doubt that the B.B.C. wartime broadcasts kept alive the spirit of resistance all over Europe and the hope of final victory over the invader.

For the proposed Royal Air Force Programme to the Luftwaffe an officer was required for liaison between Air Intelligence and the B.B.C. German Service and the Political Warfare Executive. I was designated for the job.

Until 1942 responsibility for propaganda to the enemy and occupied countries had been shared by three ministries: the Foreign Office, the Ministry of Economic Warfare and the Ministry of

Information. This was bound to cause confusion and it was agreed that the three ministers should act together through an executive committee led by Robert Bruce Lockhart, Reginald Leeper, Brigadier Brooks and Ivone Kirkpatrick, who was Controller of the B.B.C. European Services. This body would be called the Political Warfare Executive. Though announced in the Commons late in 1941, it did not achieve its final form till early in 1942 when Hugh Dalton left the Ministry of Economic Warfare and the ministers responsible were reduced to two. The Foreign Secretary looked after policy and the Minister of Information, Brendan Bracken, took over administration. He was responsible to Parliament for all broadcasting. Robert Bruce Lockhart was appointed director-general.

The propaganda makers lived at that time at Woburn Abbey, where I once visited them in the Riding School. To ensure a closer co-operation they were brought to Bush House, which was the H.Q. of the B.B.C. European Service. From then on the Political Warfare Executive and the Executive Committee controlled and administered our propaganda till the end of the war.

My job, as I understood it, was to collect suitable material from Air Intelligence, clear it from the security angle, write it up or assist the B.B.C. writers to put it into suitable form for broadcasting, attend the regular meetings of the P.W.E. committee, be prepared to speak occasionally myself in the daily programmes, advise the B.B.C. German Service in all matters relating to the R.A.F. and keep myself familiar with what was going out on other programmes e.g. the Army and Navy broadcasts and the other features which the B.B.C. was putting out in German and to know what we were saying on the leaflets we dropped on Germany and elsewhere so that we were all singing in tune and not contradicting one another.

At first I was horrified. As the only officer in the Royal Air Force authorized to speak daily to the Luftwaffe I could see that the opportunities of putting my foot in it were limitless. As it happened I was saved on many occasions by the wise counsels of the B.B.C. staff and by my friends in many branches of Air Intelligence. I had one definite responsibility and that was to have plenty of bright ideas and a reserve of subjects for at least seven days ahead. In fact Programme No. 1 was not allowed to go out on the air until I had shown that I had a supply up my sleeve. We did not want the German Air Force Programme, as it came to be called, to fizzle out on the third day for lack of material.

As a first step I was attached to a branch of Air Intelligence known as A.I.3a(2). One of its functions was to establish the order of battle of the Luftwaffe, the location of its units and of course its organization and supply. So far I had been concerned only with aircraft and equipment. In the course of our job we naturally obtained details of squadron markings, identification letters and numbers of individual aircraft and at times locations of units, which were of use to A.I.3a(2), but they also relied on interrogations and many other sources of information.

The senior officer was a marine biologist. Other members of the staff included the late Dr John Walker, afterwards Keeper of Coins and Medals at the British Museum, John Pope-Hennessy, later Sir John, the late Arthur Lane, Keeper of Ceramics at the Victoria and Albert, Geoffrey Barraclough, the historian, a quantity surveyor, a professional cricketer and the Vicar-General of the Province of York and Chancellor of the Diocese, Walter Wigglesworth. For a variety of talent A.I.3a(2) took a lot of beating. In many years of experience in the intelligence service of our country, I have come to the opinion that archaeologists, scientists, museum curators, historians and dons make the best intelligence officers. They have this in common that they are accustomed to gathering information from a wide variety of sources and reaching a logical conclusion. Actors, artists, poets and other literary men are just the opposite. They deal in emotions. They give to airy nothing a local habitation and a name, which is just what a good I.O. must not do.

I was given the simplest of briefs by Air Marshal Sir Richard Peck. I was to tell the truth and above all avoid any questions in Parliament. In the two years and more during which we ran these broadcasts, I saw very little of my supreme masters, the Air Marshal, on the R.A.F. side, and Ivone Kirkpatrick, the Controller of the B.B.C. European services. When I did, I had nothing but kindness and encouragement from both.

After I got over the initial fright, I realized that I had every advantage in this new job. I had the whole of Air Intelligence behind me for material, if I used it judiciously, and the professional help of the B.B.C. experts in putting it over. Some branches of Intelligence almost had apoplexy when, having coaxed some usable item out of them, I explained that it was for broadcasting to the enemy. The B.B.C. was less fussy. They wanted hot news. My job was to keep everybody happy.

We had only one row and that *was* over a question in Parliament. We were using a news item about the burial of a German pilot somewhere on the South Coast. Fortunately for me, it was my day off and I did not see the script. One of the B.B.C. script writers with the best intentions had mentioned that some R.A.F. aircraft had flown over as the funeral was taking place. The next day we had Lord Vansittart, no friend of the Germans at any time, the Minister for Information and the Minister for Air in full cry. Had the R.A.F. nothing else to do in the middle of a war than fly in salute over German funerals? It finally came down to my humble level and I was fortunately able to wash my hands of it. There was of course no question of the R.A.F. doing a fly-past in salute. It was purely fortuitous that a couple of our aircraft happened to be in the vicinity that day. The row died down and we had no more trouble.

The purpose of the German Air Force Programme was to undermine the confidence of German airmen in their leadership and at the same time proclaim the growing strength of the Royal Air Force. In our daily news bulletins we could counter the often exaggerated reports of operations put out by the German propaganda services. We would not play down or omit to mention our failures and we would not play up a minor success, but we would most certainly pull out all the stops when we had really big news. At no time would we belittle the achievements of the Luftwaffe whose airmen and aircraft we had every reason to respect. On the other hand we would not hesitate to point out weaknesses in their leadership or to exploit inter-service jealousies.

However, we had to get started. At times I thought that the war would be over before our first broadcast went out. The B.B.C. was naturally very wary and in the beginning not too sure that we on the Air Staff side would be able to produce sufficient suitable material regularly enough to keep a daily programme going. There was also a feeling on our side that the script writers at the B.B.C. should not be trusted to write their own versions of what the R.A.F. was doing. The best way to curb them of course was to provide plenty of good material and have confidence in their professional skill. In the event they did make the most of what we gave them and showed good judgement in the way in which it was presented.

I had in my turn to gain the confidence of A.I.3a(2). They were wondering what this cuckoo in their rather exclusive nest was up to and how much of their precious intelligence material was going to be thrown to the crowd of irresponsible journalists which some of them imagined the B.B.C. to be.

For the day-to-day running of the programme I had on the B.B.C. side an experienced broadcaster, who dated from 2 LO days and who was in addition a German scholar. He was assisted by three Germans, who had sought refuge in this country, and a secretary to type the scripts. We were also able to call on the services of German announcers from other programmes, former actors, journalists, lawyers and others who were also fugitives from the Nazis. Then there were English broadcasters who spoke German. Such speakers with a slight English accent were likely to be more convincing than native German announcers who risked being dismissed by the listeners as traitors.

Presiding over all the German broadcasts was the Head of the German Service, Hugh Carleton Greene, later Director-General of the B.B.C. and now Sir Hugh. After a career in journalism in Germany and other countries he had begun the war as a R.A.F. officer in A.I.1(k) but had been pulled out to do a far more useful job running the German service.

By the time I joined his band of propagandists, he had got over the period of 1940 and 1941, when our fortunes were at rock bottom and when it was no easy task to put over the idea to the all-victorious Germans that we would win in the end. In presenting the truth and demonstrating that it was the truth, he had not shirked the admission that we were in a bad way and, on the other hand, he had not been tempted to overdo the reporting of what little successes we had had. With this honest approach he had already prepared the way for us when our German Air Force Programme came along. We were more likely to be believed. For one armed service to speak to another any hint of the kind of bluff used by politicians would have been useless. We were experts talking to experts and we had to be factual. In fact we had to talk shop.

Yet while talking shop to the Germans and making it interesting enough to gain the attention and possibly the respect of our opposite numbers, we had to weave an underlying pattern of subversive propaganda, subtly demonstrating that all was not well within the German camp and that, despite their considerable achievements in the past, they could not win in the end. After all we were not there just to entertain them.

There were times later in the war when conditions were hardly more encouraging for us than they were in 1940 and 1941. At one or two of these critical periods the Air Marshal took me into his confidence and gave me an overall picture – British, German, Italian and Russian from all sources. Some of it was fairly depressing but he wanted me to know exactly how we stood. These background talks kept my feet firmly on the ground.

Hugh Greene too was a tempering influence. As a former journalist he had an ear for what was news and how to present it. He also understood the German mind, which few people do who have no knowledge of the language. He was very helpful in encouraging as well as deflating when our enthusiasm for some pet idea was carrying us too far. With this he had a sense of humour which helped when some of the P.W.E. committee meetings were getting out of hand, even though Dick Crossman was often in the chair, and also injected a human note into some of our more solemn scripts.

Until he could see the form in which the German Air Force Programme was going on the air and until he was sure that we had the full co-operation of Air Intelligence, there was no hope of that initial fanfare with which we expected to amaze the Luftwaffe. He was impatient at times with Air Intelligence as indeed Air Intelligence was with him. He was not always aware of what was going on, as he had no access to Air Staff matters. On the Air Staff side, as I have mentioned, they were sometimes inclined to look on the B.B.C. as a crowd of lunatic publicists clamouring for State secrets to throw away on a momentary headline. Thus I had to hold a balance, extracting good news material from the Air Ministry while assuring the more security-minded that the people in the B.B.C. were professionals who knew their job.

In general, it worked. In the end I had the officers in A.I.3a(2) thinking up ideas for us and putting aside titbits of intelligence for the B.B.C. Later it was arranged that a member of the B.B.C. staff should attend occasional meetings at the Air Ministry. This worked so well that he married one of our WAAF Intelligence Officers and I went to their wedding.

Our first problem, once the stock of ideas and material was assured, was the actual form of the programme. We had many dummy runs before the final shape of the programme was fixed. The most important point was the bait. It was decided to give in the course of the programme news of German aircrews shot down over England. If the Luftwaffe knew that they would be hearing on the following day what had happened to Hans or Fritz or Gusti missing during the night somewhere over Britain, they would listen. Even more we could count on parents and wives of men operating over Britain to turn the set on to our wave-length.

These "News of Crews" would be interspersed throughout the programme to maintain interest. If we had six names, we would announce them two at a time, between other items. There would be an opening announcement, the form of which remained unchanged. This would be followed by the news and a statement that later in the programme news would be given of airmen shot down during the previous night. Then we would have a talk lasting four or five minutes. These talks covered all manner of subjects. They might be technical, strategic or scientific. They might relate to an anniversary or to a statement by Hitler which had been proved false by current events. After the talk there would be more news of aircrews, followed by a signing-off announcement. The programme lasted a quarter of an hour.

Finally, in the autumn of 1942, came the great day. The German Air Force Programme went on the air. A voice announced, "Hier ist England! Hier ist England! Sendung der Royal Air Force. Die Royal Air Force ruft die deutsche Luftwaffe. Zuerst die Tagesnachrichten." (This is England! This is England! The Royal Air Force Programme. The Royal Air Force calling the Luftwaffe. First of all, the news.)

The end of the war for them: prisoners hand in their arms.

The mighty Wehrmacht in defeat; queue for the cookhouse.

General of the Army Dwight D. Eisenhower with General Bradley and General Patton inspect the horrors of a murder camp at Ohrdruf.

Albert Speer with friends soon after capture.

XVII

Ars est celare artem. This can be rendered for my purpose to mean that the best propaganda does not sound like propaganda. With our factual reporting of the daily news, our frank discussions of matters of mutual interest such as the relative merits of German and British aircraft, the giving of credit where credit was due, the admission of our own failures and the recognition of their successes all contributed to what might be termed an air of quiet confidence. This obvious confidence in ourselves probably achieved more than all the fanfares, boasting, accusations and the distortion or taking out of context of facts popularly associated with the word propaganda. By showing confidence in our own situation and in the strength of our own air forces, we could leave it to the enemy listeners to draw their own conclusions as to the eventual outcome of the war.

As soon as propaganda is mentioned, there is a rush from the P.R. boys, the advertising experts and the head-shrinking confraternity with their gimmicks, theories and statistics, coupled with a strong desire to get in on the racket, all demonstrating "scientifically" how you can put it over on the enemy. In time of war, the normal trade of these eager beavers falls away, so they want a job anyhow. In addition they are convinced that those already engaged on the task are the veriest amateurs and that it is time the professionals took over. Happily there were few P.R. boys at the B.B.C. and the motley collection of people recruited during the war for propaganda purposes did a good job without much experience or help from the publicity trades.

The programme once launched, my life fell into a regular routine. There were no more calls to rush out into the night to a ploughed field near Cirencester or an estuary in Yorkshire to climb over oil-spattered wreckage. I abandoned my gum boots, overalls and cameras and took over a typewriter. I dwelt in the Air Ministry and made a daily visit, sometimes two, to Bush House, where the programme went out during the afternoon. For a time I was on my own till I was joined by Rosemary Meynell, who devilled for me and showed amazing patience and forbearing. She fished in the waters of A.I.3a(2) when I had a day off and kept the B.B.C. sweet when we had a poor catch. Without much experience of air matters she contributed a lot to the success of the German Air Force Programme. Later I had an assistant in Squadron Leader Slaughter, the patent agent from A.I.2(g), who was invaluable when we were dealing with technical matters.

I established a friendly relationship with the three Germans on the German Air Force Programme, whom I shall call Schmidt, Müller and Meyer. Schmidt and Müller were two blond Hamburgers while Meyer was dark, introspective and probably Jewish. The Hamburgers' politics had caused their departure from Germany. Meyer had probably left because of his religion. He had been a sergeant in the German Air Force in the first war and he knew something about aircraft. Relations between the various Germans employed at the B.B.C. were an interesting study. There was little co-operation among them and much jealousy. Some of this was due to difference in social status. There were lawyers and actors who mixed very little with the Schmidt, Müller and Meyer class. I had to be friends with all of them and, as an outsider and an Englishman, I found this possible. But there was an atmosphere of "Don't you take any notice of *him*!" whenever I referred to the opinions of one of the others. However, there was no doubt that the B.B.C. kept them happy and got the best out of them, especially the creative writers who, I think, really enjoyed their work at the B.B.C.

I had to be familiar, as I have already said, with the other German programmes which were going out every day from Bush House. There was one programme involving two characters known as Kurt and Willi, which was very witty and excellent propaganda. Had I been listening in Germany, I would have been as much a fan as I was of Tommy Handley and ITMA. Then there was another one about a character known as Gefreiter (Corporal) Hirnschal, who wrote agonizingly constructed letters to his wife. You could almost see him sucking his pencil in the throes of literary composition as he addressed his worries to "Teuere Amalia, vielgeliebtes Weib!" (Dear Amalia, beloved wife!). His muddled ideas of the exhortations of the Fuehrer and the subsequent admonitions of his lieutenant were extremely funny and very subtle propaganda. This kind of thing was done of course by professional writers and was beyond the capacity of our Schmidt, Müller and Meyer. Nevertheless Schmidt, Müller and Meyer produced some very good scripts within the framework of the German Air Force Programme and were most useful in making clear to us what the average German would or would not swallow. This often led to arguments. We would have a bright idea and Meyer would say that was all very well for the British but Germans did not think like that. They were also very good at producing excellent themes of their own. Altogether we worked very well with the three Germans, unless I happened to walk in with no news of crews or with a poor subject for the next day's broadcast. Meyer would look at me very reproachfully over his glasses and wonder how I expected him to make bricks without straw. He would then settle down in a bad mood at his typewriter and write a good script off the cuff.

In these programmes my A.I.2(g) background furnished good material for scripts. We could discuss features of enemy aircraft and equipment and how quality might be affected as the war went on and certain materials got scarcer. We could also comment that it was a pity that some of these, much needed by the Luftwaffe, were being hived off for the German Navy. Known shortages could be related to our bombing which in time could affect the production of this or that material.

One of the regular features of the programme was a survey of the results of our bombing attacks on industrial targets in Germany. We never analysed the effect of such damage until we had seen the interpretations from Medmenham of photographs taken by high-flying aircraft on the following day. Then we were able to say with truth that such and such a part of the factory had been knocked out or that the railway junction at this or that strategic point was out of action.

We were not free from bombing ourselves. One day I was fortunately delayed and arrived at Bush House an hour or two later than I intended. Otherwise I might have been in the area when a bomb fell outside the Post Office next to the main entrance to Bush House in Aldwych. As I walked up from the Strand I noticed that articles of clothing were hanging on the trees near the entrance to Bush House. Apparently quite a number of people had been killed in the Post Office and on the street. On another occasion we were all at a P.W.E. meeting when a flying bomb was heard approaching. Suddenly it cut out, a sign that it was about to fall and explode. The meeting, including several of us in uniform, dived under the table. That is to say all except Duncan Wilson, later our Ambassador to Russia, who was in the chair and who stayed there. The bomb went off without any damage to our part of the building at least and we rose, rather shame-facedly, to find the chairman waiting to resume.

In a little-known corner of the Air Ministry at that time was a kind of nunnery staffed by talented young women who read the foreign Press, principally German and Italian, and translated any items of news which might be of interest to the various intelligence departments. Many of these young women had been educated abroad and were at least bilingual. They had always had a brief from A.I.2(g) on what to look out for and I continued to be a customer in my new capacity. They might well find something which I could use as a peg on which to hang a radio talk. The Mother Superior presiding over this learned cloister was Miss Wimble. A linguist herself, she exacted not only the highest standards from her charges but the best behaviour from the customers. No Abelard with a roving eye was permitted to flirt with any of the Héloïses in her care. Though I was allowed from time to time to have earnest and business-like discussions with the German and Italian readers, she preferred all transactions to go through her own hands. She was extremely competent in supplying us with much useful material for the programme. Instead of my daily paper I now read the *Voelkischer Beobachter*, the main organ of the Nazi Party, and other German dailies, which reached us through neutral sources. I also received such German propaganda magazines as *Signal* and the German aeronautical papers. The neutral Press, Swiss, Spanish, Swedish and so on, was also very useful. From the *Tauromaquia* supplements of the Spanish papers I learned all about bull fighting and became an *aficionado*. I knew all about Belmonte and Manolete and I was first with the news that El Gallo or El Soldado had been presented with the ears in the Madrid ring. Apart from these frivolities we did obtain quite a lot of useful intelligence from the foreign Press. It is surprising how much can slip through the strictest censorship. In the early days of A.I.2(g) we relied a lot on photographs of enemy aircraft in action before we had a plenteous supply on the ground in Britain.

Among the many types of leaflets dropped by the R.A.F. in millions over Germany was a miniature reproduction of the *Voelkischer Beobachter* of 10th October 1941. It carried a front-page headline in red:

From:
German Talks Ed.

To:
D.Eur.B.
German Sub-Ed.
German A/T
Miss Newsome
Mrs.Lund
Duty P.A.
R.P.D.L.
S/L Slaughter (2)
Policy Editor
Miss Andrews P.I.D.
Sefton Delmer P.I.D.
File.

GERMAN AIR FORCE PROGRAMME.   777.

Sunday, 31st December 1944.

17.00
===========================

Discs required:

12PM 18293.
==============

No repeats.

==

1.Disc in studio: OPENING ANNOUNCEMENT   08"

2. Sander: "Dies ist heute die letzte Sendung der   12"
                  Royal Air Force an die deutsche Luftwaffe.
                  Wir beginnen wie üblich mit den neuesten
                  Meldungen des Tages."

3.Announcer: THE NEWS   5'00"

4.Sander: NEWS OF CREWS Nos.664,665, 666.(A/M.)   1'45"

5.Sander: "Und nun spricht ein Offizier vom Stabe   05"
                  der Royal Air Force."

6.S/L.J.Peskett: THE R.A.F. GOES OFF THE AIR   5'30"
                      Written by M.C.Sander.

7.Sander: "Sie hörten einen Offizier vom Stabe der   15"
                  Royal Air Force. Zum Abschluss unserer
                  letzten Sendung der Parademarsch der Royal
                  Air Force, gespielt von der Kapelle des
                  Bomber Kommandos."

8.Disc:
   12PM 18293.   R.A.F. MARCH PAST   1'45"

                =====================================

MCS.

The final and 777th transmission of the Royal Air Force propaganda
broadcast to the Luftwaffe, in which names of shot down German air crews
were given daily.

The great hour has struck
THE CAMPAIGN IN THE EAST IS FINISHED!
Timoschenko's and Voroschilov's Army
Groups are surrounded. Budjenny's Army
Group is broken up.
The Military End of Bolshevism.

This leaflet, dropped as a reminder to the Germans at the time of the Stalingrad collapse (February 1943), could hardly be more effective. We followed similar lines in our broadcasts. We would play part of a record of a Hitler speech, in which he had made some vain promise or threat, followed by some item in the current news which demonstrated just how much it was worth.

We had a lot of fun with Goering, who once said, "If one enemy bomb ever drops on Germany, my name is Meyer!" So Meyer he became. During the course of the German Air Force Programme we ran two broadcasts to celebrate two of his birthdays. In each we announced "Das heutige Geburtstagskind!" (Today's birthday child). The birthday greeting from the Royal Air Force took the form of a survey on the following lines – "On your last birthday, Herr Reichsmarschall, you had every reason to feel happy. You had achieved this, that and the other. But, on your birthday today things are not looking so bright." Here we gave a catalogue of the misfortunes of the Luftwaffe over the year. With a final greeting we played him off with music from the Band of the Royal Air Force. We never heard if he got the message but we enjoyed composing it.

At times we had to counter speeches by Goebbels. I was impressed by some of his talks which were monitored by the B.B.C. He must often have had the same heartening effect on Germans as Churchill's had on us in some of the darkest days. Even towards the end, when all was lost as far as the Germans were concerned, I heard one speech by Goebbels which almost convinced me they were going to win. Hitler and Goering could shout their heads off but Goebbels was an adversary to be reckoned with.

By now we had quite a large number of Luftwaffe prisoners in the cage, so we thought we would do a programme on the life of a prisoner of war camp in England. In presenting this we did not exactly expect to have a rush of Luftwaffe personnel giving themselves up for the fleshpots of prison camp life, but we felt that listeners would be interested in knowing how their captured comrades were faring. At least they would realize that it was preferable to be captured by us than by the Russians who offered few amenities to their German prisoners.

We then persuaded a prisoner to do a recording on his job in the camp. "Ich bin der Koch!" (I am the cook) he announced at the beginning of his talk and then went on to describe with relish the food which he was accustomed to prepare every day for his fellow prisoners. He did it very well and made us all wish we were prisoners of war. It was an amusing broadcast without much propaganda value but it was about food and that is always an interesting subject in time of war.

I spoke occasionally myself, announced as "a Staff Officer of the Royal Air Force" and usually did a five-minute talk on some technical matter, based on my A.I.2(g) experience, or some general aspect of the war in the air. After the Battle of Britain in 1940, there was plenty of material in the Battle of the Atlantic, the operations against our Arctic convoys and the air war across the Mediterranean. Nevertheless it was not easy to find something suitable to fill a quarter of an hour every day. One can say a lot in a quarter of an hour and the B.B.C. staff were very exigent. They maintained a very high standard and viewed with a disapproving eye anything which looked like padding in our programme.

The regular P.W.E. committee meetings at Bush House were very stimulating, often extremely amusing and productive of ideas for our programme. They were usually chaired by Dick Crossman, who managed to keep a large and very mixed gathering in order. The three services were represented by the late Donald MacLachlan, then in a naval lieutenant's uniform, an officer from the War Office and myself. Then there were civilian members from various ministries, script writers from other German programmes, the leaflet writers and the rumour mongers, since it was very important that we should all tell the same story. Among those who helped with the German Air Force Programme were Marius Goring, Hubert Gregg, Christopher Serpell and others whose names are well known today.

I now had an office in an economy-style building which had been hastily run up at the corner of Monck Street near the underground H.Q. which I used to inhabit. I was given a room at the top which I filled with a growing battery of files. I had the help of the Air Ministry typing pool and tea service. In all government departments the supply of tea is of paramount importance. I lived there happily with Squadron

Leader Slaughter and Rosemary Meynell until one morning I walked up Monck Street and noticed that the corner of the top of the building had been knocked off by a flying bomb. We were then in the midst of the V.1 season. That particular corner had been my room! I went up the stairs as far as I could and clambered over steel girders which had been uncovered by the explosion and gazed into the hole, which had been the centre of the R.A.F. propaganda war against the Luftwaffe. They had certainly scored a bull's eye. My files no longer existed, all those precious scripts had been lost to posterity and on what remained of the floor was something which looked like a large spider which had died in agony. It was my beautiful typewriter. That day we went over to Bush House to explain that the Luftwaffe had struck back and that my cupboard was bare. However, they rallied round and we got something out on the air, though we made no mention of *that* particular Luftwaffe success.

XVIII

As the war progressed and the tide turned in our favour, there is no doubt that our propaganda became more effective for the simple reason that we had established our reputation for telling the truth early on when things were going badly for us. Now we had more victories to announce for ourselves and more disasters for the enemy. I think that some of our most successful broadcasts were those reporting the ever-increasing attacks by Bomber Command on enemy industrial targets and the subsequent accounts of the actual damage.

The war in Russia was now wearing down the Germans and this gave us plenty of material which was depressing for the Luftwaffe. Their morale must have been at its lowest in the appalling climatic conditions in which they had to operate. Gone were the days when the first victorious Stukas roared over Poland. Now their aircraft were lucky to get off the ground to ferry the wounded back. In North Africa too the Luftwaffe was having a bad time, which was getting worse as we continued to cut their lines of supply across the Mediterranean. The news was working so well in our favour that we could almost afford to be charitable.

Interrogation reports from the prisoner of war camps began to show weaknesses in organization and morale in the Luftwaffe, which we were able to exploit in our daily talks. I remember one significant piece of news, which came to us either through an interrogation report or from the Norwegian underground. It was to the effect that Luftwaffe officers returning to Norway from leave in Germany were packing a civilian suit. That could only mean that they had seen the writing on the wall. It might even have been a result of our propaganda. Still, it does not do for the propagandist to be over-confident. We could only cast our bread upon the waters and hope for the best. That is all one can do in times of war. One sees no results. One can fire a gun and see a man fall down. A bomb can be dropped and up goes the factory or the bridge, but our carefully prepared scripts might have been received with ribaldry and laughter for all we knew.

I think it was towards the end of the war that the Army conducted a survey among prisoners of war to find out to what extent enemy personnel had listened to foreign propaganda and how much they had been affected by it. I had an opportunity myself of talking to German airmen after the war, including some who did remember hearing our programme. Many did listen and many dismissed it as propaganda, but there is no doubt that it was effective even if it merely provoked arguments. One man said frankly, "You just talked a lot of nonsense!" Another admitted that our knowledge of what the Luftwaffe were up to shook him rigid, to use an air force expression. One said that we had made a lot of silly mistakes but at times he had to admit that we had hit the nail on the head. Moreover he could not help wondering how we had come by some of the information we had. The Army survey, as far as I remember, was encouraging and at least reassured us that we had not been wasting our sweetness on the desert air.

Now and again we were asked to broadcast a special message. A German pilot stationed in Denmark decided one day that he had had enough of the Nazi regime. He and his family had been pro-British and apparently his family had actually aided some of our shot-down pilots on the run. So he flew his night-fighter across the North Sea almost at sea level to avoid the German radar and landed somewhere near the Wash. His aircraft was of the greatest interest to us, as it was fitted with the latest night-fighter equipment. He was naturally treated with great consideration. It appears that his family knew of his intention to desert and he asked if we would broadcast a pre-arranged message which would let his people know that he was alive and safe. We agreed, and on three separate occasions the following announcement was made on the German Air Force Programme – "Hier ist eine Sonderbotschaft für Siegfried!" (Here is a special message for Siegfried!) with a quotation from Schiller, which they would recognize somewhere in Germany.

A quotation from Schiller; somehow it brought a touch of civilization in the midst of this orgy of killing. A British pilot sending such a message would have thought up something facetious, a Tommy Handley catchword. He would never have quoted Byron or Shelley. "May has come and the trees are in bloom." Those were the words which this family were awaiting. It was not one of the great purple passages of literature but it showed that somewhere in Germany there was a family, probably one of many, which recognized a quotation from Schiller. Many there must have been who were sick to death of the tasteless, vulgar culture of the Nazis and who looked back to the Germany of Goethe, Heine and Schiller. The Germans have a great pride in their literature, far more than we have in ours. They are perhaps sentimental and at times over-dramatic, but I could not help feeling touched when I went to see what was left of Goethe's house in the ruins of the Römer in Frankfurt after the war. The house was a heap of bricks and only the doorstep was recognizable. On it stood a jam jar with a flower in it. A piece of paper was attached and on it was written, "Und neues Leben blüht aus den Ruinen" (And new life blossoms from the ruins).

The night-fighter pilot came to be known as Siegfried. He was a very pleasant young man and was occasionally let loose in civilian clothes. I was given an opportunity of taking him for a walk in the country in the hope that he might talk even more freely in relaxed surroundings. We had an agreeable conversation about all manner of things which had nothing to do with the war and I got very little out of him. As we came back, we sat down to rest in a field as a flight of American bombers went over, flying south like the cranes of Ibycus. "That is the end for us!" said Siegfried philosophically as we got up to walk home. I never saw him again nor heard if his family had received his message.

Whenever I gave a talk on the German Air Force Programme I had to be rehearsed by Schmidt, Müller or Meyer and taught how to accentuate the right points. It is difficult at first not to give the impression that one is reading a script. One must talk to the microphone and even gesticulate at it to make one's remarks sound spontaneous. Timing too is very important and over-running must be avoided so one keeps a rather nervous eye on the studio clock. Schmidt and Müller were very patient but I do not think I ever really measured up to Meyer's high standard in anything. If he wanted six names for his "News of Crews" item and I turned up with a meagre three or four, he would sigh with resignation as if it was my duty to go out and shoot down a few more.

Schmidt used to say that his only regret in leaving Germany was that he had to abandon his Alsatian dog. He was alone in the world and one day, after the war, he was found dead in his rented room in Hampstead, still alone. I met one of our German colleagues some

Norddeutsche Ausgabe
283. Ausg. / 54. Jahrg. / Einzelpreis 20 Pf.

Norddeutsche Ausgabe
Berlin, Freitag, 10. Oktober 1941

„Freiheit und Brot"

VÖLKISCHER BEOBACHTER

Kampfblatt der nationalsozialistischen Bewegung
Großdeutschlands

Die große Stunde hat geschlagen:

Der Feldzug im Osten entschieden!

Heeresgruppen Timoschenko und Woroschilow eingeschlossen — Heeresgruppe Budjenny in Auflösung

Neuer Kessel bei Brjansk

Die letzten voll kampfkräftigen Divisionen der Sowjets geopfert

Aus dem Führerhauptquartier, 9. Oktober.

Das Oberkommando der Wehrmacht gibt bekannt:

Das militärische Ende des Bolschewismus

V. B. Berlin, 9. Oktober.

Der italienische Wehrmachtbericht
Brände größten Ausmaßes in Haifa

Angriff größerer italienischer Bomberverbände auf die Petroleumbehälter und Raffinerien

Rom, 9. Oktober.

This leaflet, a miniature of the "Völkischer Beobachter" announcing on
10th October 1941 the final defeat of the Russian armies and the end of
Bolshevism, was dropped in large quantities by the Royal Air Force on
Germany at the time of the Stalingrad disaster in February 1943.

years later in his dressing room at Drury Lane but of the rest I never heard again.

Among the other propaganda programmes with which I had to be familiar were the so-called "black" broadcasts, run by Sefton Delmer who has given a full account of these in his book on black propaganda (*Black Boomerang*). His imitation "German Forces Programme", or *Soldatensender Calais* as it was called, was brilliant entertainment. He ran a number of other programmes which purported to come from behind the German lines and which attacked German morale by suggesting that there were traitors broadcasting within their gates. Whether the Germans were ever taken in by this I have no idea, but some very murky propaganda was evolved. Some people thought it was hitting below the belt to spread alarm, confusion and scandal on an unlimited scale but they were akin to those in the first war who thought the use of periscopes in the trenches and the cracking of codes unsporting. Those who excused black propaganda said we were only fighting the enemy with his own weapons. Sefton Delmer had no inhibiting regulations imposed on his activities and he enjoyed himself immensely as we all did who attended meetings where his sinister programmes were discussed. There is an imp of mischief in all of us, which the laws of slander and libel normally keep under control. We could all embroider the latest bit of scandal about Goebbels or this or that Gauleiter and many did so with schoolboy zest.

I once visited Delmer's H.Q. in the country and heard the first record of "Lilli Marlene" which had been flown in for *Soldatensender Calais* from a neutral capital. His propaganda addressed to the German armed forces more or less kept within the bounds of propriety if not of truth. He offered good tunes, heroic exhortation, messages from home inspired by captured mail and some seeds of propaganda, which probably fell on fertile ground, especially towards the end of the war. We discussed ideas for programmes together but I had to be careful not to be tempted. Beside Delmer I had to be the *chevalier sans peur et sans reproche*. Without being smug I think I can say we kept to our brief and told the truth on the German Air Force Programme. I am sure it was the best way. Any advice we had to offer to Delmer and his boys was concerned with keeping him within the limits of probability where purely air matters came into question. If you are going to speak about aircraft, it is as well to know something about the subject. Delmer was always very careful to get his facts right. I think he was less particular when it came to inventing orgies for the

Nazi bosses while the German soldiers, sailors and airmen were being pressed hard on every front. Champagne flowed freely in Berlin and Paris while the men froze before Stalingrad. Ribbentrop's son had a cushy staff job in the south of France while the bombed-out populations of German cities lived in cellars like rats – and so on.

Towards the end of 1944, the Royal Air Force had achieved such a mastery over the Luftwaffe that it was felt that we could afford to wind up the German Air Force Programme. So on 31st December at 1700 hours the Royal Air Force spoke for the last time to the Luftwaffe. It was Programme No. 777.

We made the usual opening announcement. Then Schmidt said, "This is the last transmission from the Royal Air Force to the Luftwaffe. We begin as usual with the latest news of the day." One of the German announcers read the news. It was mainly about von Rundstedt's attack in the Ardennes, which had begun on 16th December and was at last being held. The Russians were fighting in Budapest. That day R.A.F. Mosquitoes bombed the Gestapo headquarters in Oslo. The news lasted five minutes, after which Schmidt gave the names of German airmen shot down, the last of many hundreds we had reported on the programme. "And now you will be hearing a staff officer of the Royal Air Force". I then read a farewell talk written by Schmidt, in which we looked back over the past two years and the events of our slow struggle to victory, then in sight. We said more or less that the Luftwaffe was now finished and that this was therefore our last appearance. Schmidt came in again and announced, "You have been listening to a staff officer of the Royal Air Force. To terminate our last transmission, the March Past of the Royal Air Force will be played by the Band of Bomber Command!" And to the music of Sir Walford Davies, erstwhile Master of the King's Music, we all looked rather blankly at one another. We had talked ourselves out of a job.

We were not quite right about the Luftwaffe being finished. The next day there were heavy air battles over the Western front. Eight hundred German aircraft made a gallant attack on Allied airfields with a loss of over a hundred and eighty, inflicting considerable damage on our uncamouflaged squadrons. But it was their swan song. They gave us little trouble thereafter, but the Luftwaffe did remain a redoubtable enemy to the end.

PART IV

Viceroys in the Making

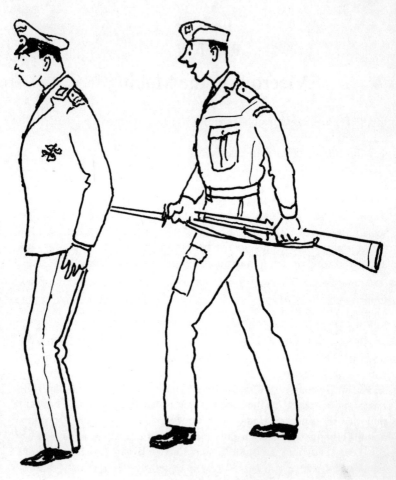

A day of extreme discomfort

XIX

In 1944 it was confidently hoped that sooner or later we would have to occupy all enemy territory and, as a beginning, preparations were well in hand for the formation of the Control Commission for Germany. On the air side it was obvious that the Royal Air Force would eventually be taking over the Luftwaffe and its installations, though none of us then had any idea of the conditions we were likely to find or how we would go about the job. It therefore behoved us to set up a Control Commission School (Air) for training officers in the form of government planned for Germany immediately after the war and in the administration and organization of the German Air Force.

A large block of flats overlooking Regent's Park and appropriately named Viceroy Court was taken over and courses were started in 1944 in the autumn. The school could accommodate two hundred officers at a time. Each course was to last a fortnight, at the end of which an examination would be held to select likely candidates for posts in Germany when the time came. As a German-speaking officer with some knowledge of the Luftwaffe, I was an obvious choice for service in Germany, so I was sent on Course No. 3 in November while I was still working on the German Air Force Programme. The large majority of officers taking these courses knew practically nothing about Germany or the Germans except as targets at the end of a gun. I had every advantage in that I had studied in Berlin long before Adolf Hitler was taken seriously, I knew the country and the language and I had been engaged on work on the Luftwaffe for over four years. I passed out at the end of my course well enough to be invited to return to the school as a lecturer. This fitted in very well with the winding-up of the German Air Force Programme. By the time I read the valedictory talk to the Luftwaffe on 31st December, I was putting future viceroys through their paces every fortnight.

The school was under the command of Group Captain (later Air

Commodore) D.M.T. Macdonald with a large staff of specialist R.A.F. officers and two Army officers. I may have thought I knew all about the Luftwaffe and Germany in general, but I was amazed at the extent of the curriculum and the thoroughness and imagination with which the job was being tackled. I found I still had a lot to learn before I could become a good teacher and I fortunately had two good teachers in the Group Captain and his deputy, Wing Commander Wilfrid Russell.

It was a hard course for most officers and covered many unfamiliar subjects. The teaching staff took groups of half a dozen to a dozen officers at a time on a wide variety of subjects, each lesson lasting about an hour. These lessons were augmented with lectures to the whole school on general subjects, given either by ourselves or visiting lecturers. Most students lived in. Work began after breakfast and went on till 6.30. Prep came after dinner so there was little time for frivolity.

The curriculum started with elementary German geography and history. I was surprised how little our students knew of the history of Europe. In English schools we have a way of teaching history in neatly wrapped-up packages entitled the Tudors, the Plantagenets, the Stuarts, the Norman Conquest and so on, not even in date order, as if nothing was happening in the rest of the world on the other side of the Channel. Few knew anything of Frederick the Great or the rise of Prussia after the Napoleonic wars. Scharnhorst and Gneisenau to them were battleships. Even the origins of the 1914 war were only vaguely understood by our generation of officers. Yet we had to show how the phenomenon of National Socialism had come about and we could not do that without reference to events in history long before the unfortunate occurrence at Braunau on the Inn in 1889. National Socialism, though bringing with it many novelties, was a logical and even unavoidable development and culmination of long-established trends in German history. Its evolution under Adolf Hitler came about at a time when circumstances were peculiarly favourable for its rapid growth and success. What Sir Neville Henderson chose to call "the blind self-confidence of a single individual and of a small clique of his followers" was by no means the only motive power which brought about the German nightmare. We had to go back therefore not necessarily to Tacitus but to the beginning of the rise of Prussia to give our students some understanding of recent German history.

I doubt if many of our officers were familiar with civil administration in our own country. These things are taken for granted and in any case the younger ones had had their time very fully taken up during the war. The next step was to give them some instruction in the civil administration of Germany and its development from the Empire of 1871 through the Imperial government and the Weimar Republic up to the seizure of power by Hitler and the complete centralization of government. This included a study of the territorial divisions of the country and the functions of government officials from the Gauleiter down to the Burgomaster of a rural parish. Associated with this we had to teach recognition of uniformed officials or *Beamten* as they were called, and their elaborate titles and insignia. Then we had to take in the complicated hierarchy of the Nazi Party with another lot of ranks and uniforms as well as the S.S. ranks and their military equivalents.

Our principal subject was of course the Luftwaffe. Here we had another set of ranks and insignia. In fact we were quite lost in the chaos of gold and silver wire, coloured collar patches, badges, decorations, tassels and little daggers with which the Germans cover their uniforms till they look like Christmas trees. Most important of all was the administration of the Luftwaffe and its chain of command which differed markedly from ours. The Luftwaffe was also responsible for A.A. Hence the two Army officers on our staff. We had a number of technical instructors to explain German aircraft and equipment. This alone was a subject for a long course but we had to cram in as much as we could.

Among the highlights of the Viceroy Court course were the distinguished visitors who came to lecture to the whole school. The talks were usually given at 5.30 for an hour, after which staff and distinguished visitor adjourned to the bar. The speakers were all of course experts on Germany and the Germans. One of the most congenial was Harold Nicolson, who spoke on the German character. His theme was that the Germans were either at your throat or at your feet. This is perhaps an over-simplification since he gave us a most penetrating study of the Germans and their weaknesses. Yet bound up with these were admirable qualities, which might lead the newcomer to think — these chaps are not so bad after all! That was the moment when you had to watch yourself. Thereafter they would interpret your kindness as weakness, your orders as requests, and you would get nowhere. They respect authority and the only way to treat them was with firmness. No philosophical discussions, no belittling of our allies, no misplaced sympathy with the condition to which they had reduced themselves by their own deeds, no fraternization and no back answers.

Some of this makes Viceroy Court sound like a hate school. But it must be remembered that the war was not yet over and it had so far been a bitter war for our survival. We had seen what had happened to other countries, we knew about Lidice and Oradour, the concentration camps and the genocide practised against the Jews and Russians, but even then the full horror of the German crimes against humanity did not appear until the final show-down at Nuremberg. What would have happened to us if they had won? Would they have allowed us to exist at all? What they did to the Poles would have been a bank holiday to the treatment we would have received. The Germans looked upon the Poles and anyone else eastwards as sub-human, but they had always envied us and with envy goes a deeper hatred. We are friends now with the new generation of Germans and another generation has grown up here, which has little idea of what we were fighting against forty years ago. Let us hope we always remain friends, but we could not be expected to be over-charitable in 1945.

If Harold Nicolson was unable to come for his periodical talk, the C.O. would ask me to go out and "give them a Nicolson". I sometimes spoke on the German character and at other times on the Germans at home as I knew them. I think I was fair. There are many German qualities which I admire but we had to point out where the Englishman, coming to Germany for the first time, might be misled.

One evening Harold Nicolson was talking to us in the bar, having just delivered his usual lecture. He was a very entertaining speaker and he was discoursing on the baroque splendours of southern Germany. For one thing he was thankful and that was that the architectural gems of Dresden had been spared. For some reason I had to go to the Air Ministry the next day and I caught a glimpse of the Operational Summary. While Harold Nicolson had been speaking in our mess, the bombs were going down on Dresden and hardly a stone was spared. Many years later, I ran into him in a restaurant and I reminded him of his words that night. "Ah, one should never say things like that!" he said and sadly walked away.

We had talks from Lord Vansittart, Lindley Fraser, a colleague on the German Air Force Programme, Wickham Steed, my former C.-in-C., Air Marshal Barratt, Ivone Kirkpatrick and other prominent figures. Lindley Fraser's subject was the political mythology of the Germans; the myth of the unbeaten army in 1918, the stab in the back by the Jews, the myth of the Allied blockade continued after the

Germans had accepted the Armistice, the myth of the Treaty of Versailles and the old story of the reparations. Then there was the Hitler mythology of the Master Race and its rights over the territories of 'inferior' peoples, the myth of Hitler's peace offer, of 'no more territorial claims' and of the wicked encirclement of Germany by jealous rivals. With his sense of humour and expressive goatee beard he was great entertainment.

Those of us who knew German gave lectures on the language but we could do little more in a short time than to give the elements of pronunciation, some key words which might prove useful, the pitfalls of German word order, some idea of road signs and the German words of command for the well-trained police dogs sometimes employed on aerodromes. German dogs could not be expected to respond if one said, "To heel, Rover, to heel!" If our students learned a few expressions peculiar to the Luftwaffe such as units and parts of aircraft, that is all we could hope for. My own minimum requirements in countries such as Lithuania, Latvia and Estonia, which I visited before the war and which have unlearnable languages, are limited to counting up to ten, saying please and thank you and knowing the differences between the Ladies and the Gents. I am afraid our future viceroys did not get much more than that from our mini German language course.

A lecture to the whole school was something of an event. One stood at the lectern, flanked by the seated figures of the Group Captain and other members of the staff. The audience ranged in rank from air commodore to flying officer. In general they were a good audience, but in every such group there is always one binder, know-all, show-off or one plain crank. You finish your lecture with your resounding final sentence and then you ask if there are any questions. This is the moment of truth. Be sure that the binder will get up, despite the fact that everyone is dying to go off to the bar, address you respectfully as 'Sir' and then bowl you a really sticky question. It always happens. Sometimes you know the answer. If you don't, the whole lecture is ruined. You have lost face. It happened to me once. I just did not know the answer. At that moment, the Group Captain saw the red light, gallantly stepped up to the lectern and said, "Would you mind if I answered that question?" and saved me.

Another important subject was that of Disarmament and Control. As part of this there was a paper on evasion and the lessons of other disarmament missions. Experience has shown that it is comparatively easy to evade armistice and surrender terms. We gave examples from the Treaty of Tilsit onwards. The history of the German General Staff and its build-up of the German Army after the 1914 war was a particularly good case in point.

The courses were originally designed for R.A.F. officers but we also had American officers occasionally among our entries. They were remarkably well informed but I had the impression that they were hand-picked for the course. However, we had one course made up of Royal Air Force N.C.O.s. I think that it was regrettable that more N.C.O.s were not trained in this way. Every officer knows how much depends on the N.C.O. in any service. While they picked up the practical side very well, they were rather at sea in the historical part of the course. The teaching staff had to mark the examination papers at the end of each course and the essays were often more entertaining than informative. One flight sergeant in his essay on the rise of National Socialism reached a culminating point with the announcement – "We now come to Charlie Main and Fred the Great". Still, some of the officers did not do much better. They may not have qualified for the history prize at Viceroy Court but they did a good job later in Germany, when they had probably forgotten all about the misdeeds of Frederick the Great.

XX

Whatever the state of the Luftwaffe when we came to take over, we had to envisage the conditions in which we might have to operate. Thus a number of practical exercises were arranged, in which a group of students under a leader would be faced with a problem of take-over or disarmament. The problem was to find a dummy unit of the Luftwaffe to disarm. This was arranged by sending a number of us, mainly teaching staff, dressed in German uniforms, to a disused R.A.F. station. We would of course speak only German. Once we were installed, the Control and Disarmament team from Viceroy Court would arrive and endeavour to take over the station. They were free to do anything they liked. After the exercise, if we survived, they would be given good or bad marks on the way they behaved and on the efficiency of the take-over. We too, the Germans, could do as we liked and get up to any tricks to frustrate the victorious R.A.F.

In this way I found myself as the Commanding Officer of a German Air Force station in one of these charades. I was dressed up and given an office, which I shared with my P.A. This was Lettice Ashley-Cooper, an old colleague from A.I.3a(2) disguised as a German WAAF officer. My men were scattered round the station engaged on various imaginary jobs and with licence to be as difficult as possible.

The take-over R.A.F. party, headed by a group captain, duly arrived and began to move in. He dispersed his men to different strategic points and then crashed into my office, calling upon me to surrender. I refused to speak anything but German and everything had to go through the interpreter. I remained stiffly at attention and gave the most unhelpful answers to all questions. I would not supply a plan of the station, I would not say where the bomb store was located, in fact I would not do anything and I resented his intrusion on my privacy. So I was marched off under arrest with two guards poking their bayonets in my back. My P.A., similarly unco-operative, was also removed while they ransacked my office.

In the meantime the rest of the heroic team from Viceroy Court had rounded up as many 'Luftwaffe' personnel as they could find and had made the mistake of putting them behind a fenced enclosure which contained the coal store. Since the imaginary Germans had permission to do as they liked, they used the coal as ammunition and pelted the invading force from the other side of the fence. There was a good deal of horseplay before order was restored. The group captain continued his interrogation but he got very little out of me. However, the team prevented any sabotage and eventually had all 'enemy' personnel under control. A good time was had by all except the prisoners and I recall the day as one of extreme discomfort. I was glad at the end to resume my own rank and function. It was a good exercise in interrogation, since most officers would have to work through an interpreter in Germany. So we gave out the marks when we got back and agreed they had not done too badly.

We held special classes in interrogation back at the school, in which one generously proportioned member of the staff played the part of a German officer. He spoke excellent German and was encouraged to be as unpleasant as possible. He had a magnificent uniform and the inevitable polished black riding boots. These exercises were conducted in the presence of the whole school. Small groups came up one at a time with a given problem, which had to be solved by getting information out of the German officer. The interpreter batted question and answer back and forth to be judged by the audience.

This was all very good entertainment but it was hard work with a strict time-table and an important examination at the end of each course. The results went on every officer's record. We wrote our own lectures, which were run off duplicators and circulated to each student, and we marked the final papers. The group captain, when he was not up to his eyes in administration, used to stroll round from class to class and sit in for a quarter of an hour, so we had to be on our toes. He also attended all big lectures and occasionally gave one himself.

Meanwhile events were moving fast. We had our own small alarms with V.1s and V.2s in the neighbourhood. Now and again lectures were interrupted and we all climbed up on the roof to see where the smoke was coming from after any particularly loud bang, but our hatchery of future proconsuls remained intact. Farther afield, the Russians were in Warsaw and soon after in Vienna. The Yalta

Conference took place. The Germans were cleared out of Belgian territory. The Americans crossed the Rhine at Remagen and 21st Army Group attacked across the Lower Rhine. The net was closing in.

Then in April 1945, the two notorious characters who opened the first chapter of this book met their end. The two beggars on horseback had reached their destination. They died within two days of one another; Mussolini shot by partisans while on the run on 28th April, and Hitler by his own hand in the shabby Götterdämmerung of his underground hide-out on the 30th. There was many a dry eye when those two were gathered to Beelzebub's bosom.

For us the time for play-acting and going through the motions was over. At the beginning of May came the unconditional surrender and the job for which we had all been preparing was waiting for us. No more imitation German officers, no more theoretical problems. This was the real thing and Heaven only knew what we were going to find when we got to Germany. When the school was wound up, I thought my job was done, but it was pointed out to me that, having been telling people for so long how to occupy Germany, it was only logical that I should have a shot at it myself. I did not realize that I was to spend the next two years in Germany.

I had held the rank of squadron leader for some time, so I was promoted to wing commander. Early in July I climbed into the empty fuselage of a DC 4 at Northolt and, after a flight lasting almost as long as a present-day trip to New York, I landed at the German Air Force station at Detmold.

PART V

Fiddler's Paradise

On 14th July "fraternisation" became legal

XXI

It was July 1945 and Friday the 13th. As I landed I thought of the German triumphal entry into Paris just over five years earlier, of the bands and the arrogant jackboots stamping down the Champs Elysées. We did not march into Germany as conquerors; we slipped in almost apologetically to take over the mess which Hitler had left behind. I had never imagined myself crowned with the victor's laurels marching through the Brandenburg Gate in Berlin. In fact we were concerned during most of the war to prevent a procession of German jackboots through the Admiralty Arch up the Mall. So here I was among the damaged hangars of Detmold, a most unromantic setting as the climax or rather anticlimax of five years of blood, sweat and tears.

There was nothing to detain me in Detmold so I was driven off straight to Lübbecke, a pleasant little town of no distinction whatever lying to the west of Minden, the Porta Westfalica. Here in Lübbecke was the intelligence headquarters to which I was attached. For the last two miles of the journey through a pleasant undulating countryside with tree-covered hills, notice boards on trees announced that we were approaching Control Commission Headquarters.

Our part of the town was fenced off with barbed wire and the only Germans allowed within our enclosure were servants who had to carry a pass. The locals were glad of a job, as it meant rations and employment, both extremely scarce at that time. We worked and lived in little houses taken over from families, who were moved out at short notice with only what they could carry. Lübbecke was remote from any industrial area or fighting zone so there was practically no war damage.

Our intelligence unit, rather thinly disguised as a liaison group, was commanded by an elderly colonel and the staff was made up of Army officers, apart from myself, aided by other ranks as orderlies and clerks. We had a bevy of secretaries in F.A.N.Y. uniforms. Everyone going to Germany had to wear uniform. Even the Ballet Rambert, on a visit to entertain us, wore uniform when they were not prancing about in their tutus. Our girls, under their curious designation as First Aid Nursing Yeomanry, looked very attractive. They were not nurses and they bore no resemblance to yeomanry but they were one up on the girls in the civilian part of the Control Commission, who wore a less glamorous khaki with green tabs. The male civil servants also wore khaki but with no badges of rank. Nevertheless they were very conscious of what was known as their equivalent rank. A civilian of a certain status in Whitehall might be equated to the rank of major or colonel, but would not be addressed by that rank. Later it was said that the equivalent rank granted to the hangman at Nuremberg was that of brigadier. However, that is no reflection on the civilian officers of the Control Commission for Germany, who somehow managed to bring order out of chaos in situations undreamed of in their tidy little offices at home.

I spent one day settling in and driving over to Bad Salzuflen, which was to be my home later on. The next day being Sunday, we ceased governing Germany and had a day off. I decided to have a look at the Pied Piper's town of Hameln. We drove by way of Minden, where we were unable to cross the Weser as the main bridge was down and we missed the temporary bridge. We went on to Vlotho where a very masculine and efficient Red Cross female told us the bridge there was also blown and directed us via Rinteln to Hameln along the Weser bank. On the way we passed the red-roofed Schloss Schaumburg high on a wooded hill. We crossed lower down the river on a small bridge which barely allowed enough head room for the car. Thus we came to Hameln. For months all our journeys were constantly frustrated and considerably lengthened by blown bridges and diversions. Everywhere one saw the sign UMLEITUNG (diversion). One week-end we lent some of the men a car to tour round the country. When my own batman returned, I asked him where he had been. He replied that they had been to a place called UM-LEE-TUNG but they 'didn't think much of it'.

Hameln fulfilled all my expectations with its Walt Disney houses dating from the sixteenth and seventeenth centuries. Many were ornamented with texts from the Bible. It was also customary in this and many other towns of this area to inscribe over the main door of the house the name of the original owner and that of his wife. All the wooden parts of the façade of the houses are richly carved and painted in bright colours. As many as five storeys rise to a gracefully pointed gable. There is a particularly fine one in Bad Salzuflen, to which Pastor Johan Loofher brought his bride, Anna Resen, in 1621. Over the high and wide door is the inscription − JOHAN LOOFHER et ANNA RESEN. For forty years he was pastor there and his life fulfilled the wish carved in Latin right across the housefront − "May lasting harmony be granted to those who dwell herein and may the soft firelight ever illuminate their hearth. The Lord will provide." He survived the rigours and miseries of the Thirty Years War so it could not have been easy going. Such inscriptions and the loving care lavished on these houses gave one a glimpse of a Germany far removed from that of Adolf Hitler.

I confirmed that the River Weser was deep and wide as it washed the walls of Hameln on its southern side. New generations of children have grown up since the Pied Piper took the Hameln children of over six hundred years ago into Koppelberg Hill, when that wondrous portal opened wide. Dozens of them were bathing in the river where some tree trunks were moored to form a swimming pool.

One part of the main bridge was blown up to remind us that we were in 1945. The gap was filled with a temporary construction made from the wreckage of the blown part so that pedestrians had to climb down to make the crossing. There was a very large factory on the south bank destroyed by bombing and there was damage to a large church on the north side. Another church in the town was burnt to a shell but the memorial stones in the walls were still legible.

Hameln is a town of fine wide streets and avenues but in the old part of the town the streets are narrow and full of picturesque houses, each with its mural inscription. I found no statue of the Pied Piper and I wondered if the whole story had been an invention of Robert Browning. However, on what is called the Ratcatcher House is a stone inscription in old German:

Anno 1284
Am Dage Johannis et Pauli
War den 26. Junii
Dorch einen Piper mit allerley Farve bekledet
Gewesen CXXX Kinder verledet
Binnen Hamelen geborn
To Calvarie bi den Koppen verloren.

Thus it is recorded that in the year 1284 on the Feast of St John and St Paul, which was the 26th of June, one hundred and thirty children born in Hameln were led away by a piper clad in many colours and lost on that hill outside the town. There is a similar memorial on the Hochzeitshaus or Marriage House, another fine building of the early seventeenth century.

Before leaving, we offered our army driver the opportunity of a stroll round the town while we stayed in the car. In those days one never left a car unattended. He showed not the slightest interest and somehow this made me feel very sad. So we took the road back. Here and there tanks, A.A. guns and wrecked motor vehicles lay by the roadside – mostly German.

This time we drove through Bückeburg, at one time the residence of the Princes of Schaumburg-Lippe. Here we saw women in their picturesque regional costume, over which they wear a long black cloak. We stopped to look at the elaborately decorated façade of the Baroque Lutheran church and at the organ, on which one of the Bachs had played. I was not able to establish which one. As Bach had twenty children – quite a feat when one considers the volume of his musical works – the uncertainty is quite understandable.

Minden was badly damaged in parts and some streets were hopeless masses of rubble. However, it was nothing to what we were to see later in other German towns. It was here at Minden on 1st August 1759 that one of the most memorable battles of the Seven Years War was fought, a battle in which British troops distinguished themselves with courage and determination comparable with the glories of Waterloo. As at the great trial of strength over half a century later, it was infantry fire power which prevailed over cavalry and which drew from the enemy commander, the Marquis de Contades, the remark that he "never thought to see a single line of infantry break through three lines of cavalry ranked in order of battle and tumble them to ruin". The colours of six British infantry regiments bear the battle honour "Minden" and the battle is commemorated every year on Minden Day. I was unfortunately not able to be in Minden on 1st August 1945, when I heard that the usual celebration was to take place where the battle was actually fought. It is a battle to be remembered for another good reason; the second-in-command and one who made a great contribution to the victory that day was Lieutenant-General the Marquis of Granby, whose name adorns many a public house to this day.

Along the road we met demobilized German soldiers and occasionally sailors and airmen on the long tramp home. These scarecrows were a far cry from the proud army which had marched down the Champs Elysées. In the towns many of the men had to continue to wear their uniforms for lack of civilian clothing. Badges of rank had been removed and replaced by a greenish-yellow triangle on the breast pocket to show that they had been demobilized. There were no Nazi symbols or signs to be seen anywhere. It was difficult to believe that the Party had ever existed. The only reference to Hitler was in the oft-repeated scrawl on the walls of wrecked buildings – "Zwölf Jahre hat Hitler dazu gebraucht!" With bitter memories of the promised Thousand Year Reich, the Germans thus proclaimed that it had taken Hitler only twelve years to bring them to destruction.

So far I had seen very little of the horrors of war in Germany. The countryside looked peaceful and every inch of land seemed to be cultivated. The villagers were healthy and well-fed and it appeared that this little corner of Westphalia had suffered very little. By the time I left Germany, however, I had travelled all over the country from Aachen to Berlin and from Hamburg to Frankfurt and Nuremberg and had seen what a country looks like when it is flat on its back.

Before the final surrender, the government had been that of the National Socialist Party and that clearly no longer existed. In fact, on the day of my arrival in Germany, it was officially announced by the Berlin municipal council that it had decided to confiscate the property of all members of the National Socialist Party and those who had "reaped benefit from the National Socialist Party, state, army or economy". That meant practically everybody holding public office during the war. Thus government had broken down and the administration of this enormous area had been taken over by the Control Commission. It was a stupendous task, the difficulty of which can hardly be realized today. It would take a far larger book than this even to begin to describe the complexity of the job facing the military and civilian organizations which we had to provide to avoid further disaster. The Germans are not good at improvising. They need order and authority. Both Military Government and the Control Commission had to establish both. This was complicated at first by the setting up of four separate zones; British, French, American and Russian. The Russian remained Russian throughout and there was no relaxation there, but in the other three zones administration and attitudes to the population varied and the Germans were quick to play off one against the other. Germans in our zone would be critical and scornful of the French in the hope of currying favour with us or they would deride the laxity of the Americans. Rations among the Americans were far better than those of our own troops and a German who could get a job with them was generally better off than he would be with us. The French were understandably tough. They had had four years of German occupation.

From the German point of view it could be a fiddler's paradise and that is what occupied Germany became. When you have no job, no home and all the shops are closed, you have to devise some way of keeping alive. You become a fiddler and fiddling begets fiddling. The usual black markets developed and naturally involved the occupiers as well as the occupied. Many Germans possessed goods we had lacked for years and we had food, clothes, tyres, petrol and everything they needed to keep going. In our area of Westphalia there was of course country produce and shortage of the basic food products was not so pronounced. In the towns and cities, however, theft, barter and every other kind of fiddle became the order of the day. Even at high official levels there had to be a *quid pro quo*. If you do this, we will provide the necessary material and so on.

Fortunately for me, I had no part or responsibility in problems of administration save the minor headaches of accommodation and servants. As an intelligence officer I had to observe and report. That meant a lot of travelling and meeting people all over Germany. The civilians in the Control Commission were mostly cooped up in offices, smothered with papers and with all the frustrations of language difficulties, trying to build up a government from scratch. So once again, as in France in 1940, I found myself in the happy position of being able to go where I pleased. Speaking German, I had no need of an interpreter and hence there were fewer misunderstandings in my dealings with Germans.

XXII

One of my first tasks was to go down to Brussels and I set off with my driver on the Hanover-Hamm autobahn, which passes south-west of Herford over the Teutoburger Wald, where the German tribes under Armenius, called by the Germans Hermann, destroyed the Roman legions of P. Quintilius Varus in the year A.D. 9. This event, as we used to teach in the Control Commission School, effectively denied the savage Germans the benefits of Roman civilization. Our aircraft flying into Germany at the time I was there used to pass over the gigantic statue of Hermann, the Hermannsdenkmal as it is called, which stands on the crest of a hill called the Grotenburg near Detmold. Even from the air it is a most impressive sight. There he stands, his twenty-foot sword held high, defying the invaders. On his sword is the inscription:

Germany's unity is my strength,
My strength is Germany's power!

Well might he have cried, as Augustus Caesar cried to Varus, "Give me back my legions!"

There was a lot of traffic going up the autobahn. We passed lorry-loads of demobilized Germans and agricultural machinery being taken up under the 'Barleycorn' scheme for recruiting labour for the harvest that year. There were very few private cars. One impression of the autobahn anywhere in Germany in those days was of innumerable little green beetles crawling along, as the Volkswagens of the Control Commission went about their business. There was only one model of Volkswagen in those days and a very useful model it was. I was now to see what German refugees looked like, as lorries packed with as many as thirty or forty German civilians, complete with Grandma at the back, plus trailers full of household goods, trundled along at five miles an hour. From such travellers we received quite understandably some very surly looks.

At most places where the autobahn passed over a viaduct – and this applied all over Germany – one arch had been blown up. This meant that Bailey bridges had to be put across for one line of traffic and we were constantly slowed down into single lines. Many of the bridges bore a title such as 'Victory Bridge' and a notice to the effect that it had been built by this or that company of Engineers.

We drove off the autobahn at the entrance to Dortmund. We had to negotiate a steep track and finally turn into a road leading into the complete devastation of that city. As we approached the centre the bomb damage got worse. It was a spectacle of complete destruction. I was to see many such sights all over Germany and I was always reminded of the oft-repeated quotation from Macaulay – "When some traveller from New Zealand shall, in the midst of a vast solitude, take his stand on a broken arch of London Bridge to sketch the ruins of St Paul's." How near had we been to that very scene. It first came into my mind when I saw the ruins of Cologne. As far as the eye could see in any direction was a desert of white rubble and dust in the summer sunshine. The green girders of the Hindenburg and Hohenzollern bridges lay in the waters of the Rhine and somehow majestically the two great black spires of the cathedral stood up out of the desolation, the black contrasting sharply with the white dust. To me it looked like the end of the world. A few days later a bomb was to be dropped at Hiroshima, which would utterly destroy four square miles of the city and practically wipe out the whole population. Dortmund was my first experience of such destruction and it came to me as a shock just as my first sight of a dead German airman did near La Bassée back in 1940.

We had to make our way in Germany then in single-line traffic through lanes cleared in the rubble. Often these tracks and roads leading into towns were marked "Shoulders cleared of mines for 10 yards." It was certainly an occasion for keeping to the straight and narrow path.

Where large factories and blocks of dwellings had stood were heap upon heap of brickwork with gaunt walls and chimney stacks in all directions. For long distances there was not a single habitable building to be seen. Most of the ruins were untouched and only the main roadways had been cleared. Trams were overthrown, track torn up and everything had been left where it fell. At the principal railway stations one saw the skeletons of burnt-out trucks and waggons with the wreckage of tanks and aircraft still in them. The girders of the station roof had often collapsed across the chaotic mess.

Yet through the desolate wilderness the people of Dortmund walked, incredibly clean and apparently well nourished. Where they lived, slept and washed was a complete puzzle. Girls wore spotless white or light-coloured dresses unaffected by the haze of dust which hung over destroyed towns like Dortmund. Neatly dressed businessmen hurried along with little leather briefcases under their arms, though God knows what business they had to do or where they were going to find it. The only indication of any difference in their mode of living was that one occasionally saw a woman with a pail on the way to some communal tap or pump for water. I could only conclude that they all lived underground somewhere in air raid shelters or in holes in the ground like the marmots in Switzerland.

Somehow in these surroundings I felt an intruder. Peace and victory had seemed so remote throughout most of the war period and we had been so preoccupied with not being defeated that we had little time to imagine what it would be like to conquer. We had seen "To Berlin" written on railway carriages at the beginning of both world wars and had possibly imagined ourselves storming into German cities in a flurry of flags but this had soon been forgotten in the worries of rations, coupons, sirens, black-outs and the simple business of keeping alive. It was hard to adjust oneself to the role of conqueror. Rape and pillage were far from my mind as I watched this rather stuffy urban population going about its invisible business. I did not hate them. In fact I could not help admiring their courage, fanaticism, resignation or whatever else enabled them to stand up to such bombing as we had never known in Britain. There was quite definitely a feeling of intrusion, especially when we had to occupy their houses, use their furniture and read their books. It was like calling on someone when it was highly inconvenient for them, in the midst of spring-cleaning or when they had the drains up. Once the Germans realized that we had no intention of lining them up against the wall and shooting them or throwing their babies up in the air and catching them on our bayonets, they mostly settled for a life of peaceful co-existence with us as a source of cigarettes, bars of chocolate and above all a pound of coffee. I suppose we could have inspired fear and imposed good behaviour by rampaging through the towns with a sword in one hand and a revolver in the other — King's Regs forbade it anyway — but with a pound of coffee and a few tins of sardines you could have the whole population feeding out of your hand. All in all, I felt rather apologetic about being there at all. I certainly could not imagine that this lot of solid bourgeois had at one time screamed themselves hoarse when the shabby little man in the raincoat had told them they were the Herrenvolk and masters of the whole world. Lots of these smug businessmen had been wearing a uniform of some kind not long before, all covered with swastikas, shouting orders to others in less splendid uniforms, who in their turn were driving the enslaved peoples of most of Europe.

There was little *dolce vita* to keep us in Dortmund and we drove on through Essen, Düsseldorf, Cologne and Düren, where the same pattern of destruction was repeated. I had never before been in Aachen, which was the next town on our route. Here was the city of Charlemagne, its cathedral one of the oldest churches of Christendom. Here was the destination of Browning's mysterious rider who brought the good news from Ghent. What a disappointment! The usual rubble and mess everywhere. I was shown one road which ran down a slope to a small square. During the fighting there, a tram loaded with explosives had been released with its brakes off to run down the slope and explode in the square. Near by a statue of Bismarck stood on a high plinth undamaged among the surrounding flattened buildings. The signals engineers had been unable to find a building or lamp post on which to fix their telephone wires, so they were all strung round Bismarck's neck, from which army communications radiated in all directions.

Finally, over the Dutch border through Maastricht, Hasselt, Diest and Louvain, we came to Brussels, a city I had known well since 1923. After wartime Britain it looked surprisingly prosperous. If you know where to go in Brussels, it is a gourmet's paradise at any time, but in the immediate post-war period the presence of British troops called for one single dish. In almost every café and restaurant there was a sign – Egg and Chips. In the great conquests of olden days, I had always imagined, aided by pictures of roistering invaders, from the Mongol hordes to the Nazis in Paris, that one plundered the richest viands and finest wines of the conquered country. Yet our warriors, fighting their way from the sands of El Alamein along the North African coast through the Sicily and Anzio landings and up the Italian peninsula to the heart of Europe, or, seasick from the Normandy landings, plunging up the beaches and on through France to the Rhine, had taken no heed of the Camembert and Brie, had disdained the *pâté de foie gras* of Strasbourg, had beaten the enemy to a standstill and finally demanded – Egg and Chips!

There was no Customs barrier between Germany and Belgium – at least I never found one – so the highroad from Brussels to Berlin became one of the main routes for fiddlers. There appeared to be supplies of food and other consumer goods in plenty in Belgium, which could be exchanged against equipment of various kinds from Germany. If one's unit in Germany was still feeding on tinned M. & V. (meat and vegetables), a peculiarly odious concoction, a set of tyres could be "flogged" in Brussels for a greatly improved diet. Where you got the tyres was nobody's business. Should anyone be unwise enough to leave his car out overnight, he might well find it bereft of tyres on the morrow. Petrol could be siphoned out of cars just as it was among the motoring refugees on the retreat south in 1940. Even after the catharsis of a great war, the human race does not improve.

In poor old England, we were still being rationed into the fifties and I never went home on leave without taking a supply of food to victorious Britain from little oppressed Belgium.

Anyone who wanted a good time in Brussels could save up his NAAFI ration of liquor or procure a few bottles of German gin – I think it was called Steinhäger – and go along to a bar or night club which was short of strong drink. A couple of bottles would pay for the food and the evening's entertainment. The German gin was not to everybody's taste but it could be disguised in a cocktail. Girls from the Control Commission offices who had scarcely come off their mother's milk became addicted to B and B, a mixture of brandy and Bénédictine.

Back in Germany we were coming to terms with the population. There had been one upset about the relaxation of the order forbidding what was curiously termed fraternization. This was no matter of brotherly love but rather of the desires of the flesh. Among our licentious soldiery, an attractive German girl would be described as 'a nice bit of frat', which shows how a word can go astray in a language. When we were hemmed in by barbed wire and any association with Germans was prohibited, love could spring up in the hearts of the occupying warriors and the German maidens. With innumerable young German soldiers still in Russian captivity, the fräuleins were not too unwilling. As I have pointed out elsewhere, a foreign uniform works wonders, even if it is that of the recent enemy. In addition, cigarettes and bars of chocolate gave our troops a considerable advantage over the unemployed local German males. But, when the German population heard of the order that, as from Saturday, 14th July, (why Bastille Day?) the fraternization ban was solemnly modified in the British and American Zones of Germany and Austria, the fräuleins took it rather badly and we almost had a Lysistrata situation on our hands. Our men reported a sudden coolness — since a certain amount of 'fratting' had already taken place, stolen fruit being the sweetest — and for a brief period there was general consternation. However, human nature triumphed in the end and in a short time all was well again. This was inevitably tied up with trade. Cigarettes and bars of chocolate went a long way to cement the bonds of affection between occupiers and occupied.

The British soldier, true to the tradition of 'Wipers' for Ypres in 1914, had his own pronunciation for the names of German towns. Thus Lübbecke became Loobecky and Bünde rhymed with Monday. We took over a local country house called Schloss Mengersen where we could spend week-ends and relax. The little houses in Lübbecke were all right as offices and sleeping quarters but Schloss Mengersen offered spacious rooms and pleasant grounds. 'Schloss' was one word which our troops failed to master and our week-end home came to be referred to as the 'Slosh'. 'Going up the Slosh' meant a trip to Schloss Mengersen. The owner of this house, Baron Mengersen, was at first allowed to live in the porter's lodge, but he was in the habit of criticizing our way of life and for ever keeping an eye on his furniture, so he had to be removed elsewhere. His housekeeper was more amenable. She lived on the premises and 'did' for us. I never knew her name, as she was always called Gestatten Sie! (Allow me!) from her habit of prefixing every remark with this polite phrase. Little did the Baron or, for that matter, the military authorities know that our men had secreted a 'liberated' calf in the cellar. Nothing was ever stolen. It was just liberated. This beast, together with a large pig, who dwelt at the back of our transport yard at Bad Salzuflen, eventually augmented our rather monotonous rations at that time. If by some unhappy chance or deliberate intent one ran over a chicken or a turkey while driving through a village, it was duly collected, mangled as it was, for the pot that evening. Strictly speaking we were not allowed to live on the country in the true Napoleonic manner but there were no rules against hunting. All firearms, including sporting guns, had had to be given up and they were usually stored at the local police station. Thus one of the younger officers could be told off to go down and borrow a gun and try his luck with anything from venison to the odd hare or pheasant. These activities were varied by expeditions into the Teutoburger Wald with a view to clearing ski slopes for the coming winter.

XXIII

Our relations with the French had understandably not been exactly cordial in 1940. During the war we had had our ups and downs. What with Oran, Admiral Darlan, Dakar and General de Gaulle there was plenty of room for disagreement up to outright hostility, though I myself have a pleasant memory of Admiral Muselier at Carlton House Terrace and of friendly contacts with French officers whenever I met them. I am sure it was mainly because I spoke French and had some understanding of their mentality. This again served me in good stead among the French in Germany.

In London on leave I had made the acquaintance of a man who before the war had imported wines from the Nierstein district of the Rhine. He suggested that I might look up one or two of his old suppliers, so on one of my visits to Frankfurt to set up a liaison with the Americans, I took the opportunity of calling on the two vineyards of Schmitt and Guntrum. I found that they were not permitted to sell their wines in Germany or export them. The vineyards came under the supervision of the French Military Government at Mainz, then referred to as Mayence. I was told that the only way I could get my hands on any of their wines was with a *bon de déblocage* or clearance note to be obtained from the officer in charge there. That is how I came to make friends with Capitaine Israël at Mayence. From him I could always count on a *bon* for two hundred bottles at a time of the finest vintages in Germany. As the price was about two shillings a bottle I was very popular with the Mess Secretary back in Bad Salzuflen. When I used to call on Capitaine Israël, there was usually an enormous queue of Germans outside his office to ask favours, but they all had to wait when I was announced. One can well imagine that, with a name like Israël, he was not unduly considerate in his dealings with the Germans. This will be even more readily understood from the following story.

Capitaine Israël's brother René had been an officer of the Free

French Forces in England and he had been parachuted into occupied France. Unfortunately he broke both legs on landing and was cared for in captivity by French nuns. Knowing that, as soon as he could walk again, he would probably be shot, they kept his legs in plaster longer than necessary. This did not please the Gestapo who finally lost patience and had him carried down to a courtyard, where he was propped against the wall and executed.

Reporting in London on leave from Germany, I was asked to take back to the French Zone of Germany a kitbag containing René Israël's uniform, decorations and other personal possessions which he had left in London before his last mission over France. I later arrived at the office of Capitaine Israël with his brother's effects. These I handed over with the usual expressions of condolence and was invited to lunch at the French mess. Here I met a large number of French officers and their wives, for, unlike the British forces in Germany, the French had been allowed to have their families with them.

At the end of a delightful lunch, I was asked if there was anything they could do for me as some token of thanks for the service I had rendered in bringing back their comrade's belongings. There was a well-known singer among them whose name I do not recall, and there was a piano at the end of the room. I asked if he would sing "Le Fiacre", the song made famous by Jean Sablon. This he did and it went some way towards brightening an otherwise rather sad occasion.

When I left, my car was waiting for me at the main entrance. There was much hand-shaking and saluting and at the last minute, two orderlies arrived bearing a large wooden case to be loaded into the boot of my car. The lid was lifted to show me the contents. It was a typical French gesture and beautifully timed. The case was packed with bottles of wine, one bottle each from all the great wine-growing districts of France. In this way these kindly French people demonstrated their appreciation of our returning the uniform and decorations of their dead comrade.

The wines which I regularly brought from the French Zone for the mess were the best which the vineyards of Nierstein and Oppenheim could supply. I was always made welcome by the families of Schmitt and Guntrum. They were people who looked back on many centuries of wine-growing. They too had lost brothers and other relatives in the war and it was sad to think that the people who produced such good wine on one side of the Rhine had had to go to war with those who had given me the best of the provinces of France up at Mayence.

Frankfurt was a popular trip for us. The Americans, welcoming as usual, gave us the run of the P.X., which meant access to foods and consumer goods which we had not seen for five years. The city was badly damaged by bombing, though not as badly as some other places in Germany. It was ironical to see inscribed on the façade of the damaged opera house – "To the True, the Good and the Beautiful", when very little that was any of these things had been seen in Germany since 1933.

In the hotel where I stayed I decided to have a bath.

When I turned on the tap, there appeared a malodorous dark brown fluid suggesting that the sewage and the water supply had somehow got mixed up, so I had to wait for a bath till I got back. The American drivers on the roads terrified me more than anything else I had experienced throughout the war. That they were good drivers there is no doubt but they must have suffered more casualties from speeding than they ever did in battle. The American authorities realized this and the most awful warnings were posted everywhere. They even erected at danger points or at places where a serious accident had happened plinths of stone, on which wrecked jeeps or cars were placed complete with artificially blood-stained dummies in uniform. A skull and crossbones and "THIS COULD BE YOU!" or "DEATH IS SO PERMANENT!" was the message, which of course was unheeded.

It was a pleasant drive down to Frankfurt, apart from the hazards of American driving. We went through Paderborn and Arolsen past the Eder dam to the university town of Marburg and on through Giessen. From Frankfurt I used to make trips to Mayence for my *bons de déblocage* and once I went down the Rhine to Koblenz to see the great fortress of Ehrenbreitstein overlooking the confluence of the Rhine and the Moselle. I was shown over the fortress with its fantastically thick walls on which the tricolour was flying triumphantly over the great statue of the Emperor William I, standing at the German Corner, as it is called, where the two rivers join.

About the middle of August, I had to go to Berlin. This was the moment I had been waiting for. It was a long and tedious journey with the usual delays where the autobahn had been damaged. We passed the Russian check-point at Helmstedt without difficulty and thereafter had to keep going.

We were to put up at an undamaged house – there were not many – in the western suburbs, but I wanted to get to the centre of the city without delay that same day. I had studied in Berlin in 1926 and paid occasional visits later before the war and now I wanted to see it after the Four Horsemen had passed over it. It so happened that my car needed attention and I had no other transport. Then a despatch rider, hearing that I wanted to get to the Brandenburg Gate, offered to take me on his motorcycle. He deposited me close to the Brandenburg Gate with my nerves in shreds, promising to send a car later to pick me up. Nothing on earth would have tempted me to get on that motorcycle again.

My army batman had asked me to procure a camera for him if I saw one for sale. I had one of my own so I did not need one myself. As I walked towards the wreck of the burned-out Reichstag and the Brandenburg Gate, a man came up to me with a very nice Voigtländer camera and said it was for sale – or rather for barter. I said, "What do you want?" and he replied that he would settle for cigarettes, which were by then the universal currency. As it happened, all I had in my pocket was a packet of ten and a twopenny bar of chocolate. Yes, in those days a bar of chocolate did cost two old pence and ten cigarettes cost six. I said that I regretted that this was all I had on me, but the man jumped at the bargain and I found myself in possession of a new camera with an unused film in it. I then went on a hundred yards or so to be confronted with an enormous notice announcing that it was strictly forbidden for service personnel to engage in barter deals by order of the Military Government. I looked round and prayed that no M.P. had seen a Royal Air Force officer flogging his cigarettes for a German camera. I had only been thinking of doing my batman a good turn. Anyway, when I got back, I sent for him, told him to produce ten cigarettes and a bar of chocolate, which he did with some surprise. I then gave him his camera with a severe reprimand for engaging in barter, especially through the intermediary of an officer, and told him to forget the whole transaction. Thus I salved my conscience and he of course was delighted.

However, there I was at last in the centre of Berlin, having narrowly escaped being arrested for illegal barter within a minute or two of my arrival. In 1972 the B.B.C. put on a T.V. feature on the theme of what would have happened if we had lost the war. It was not very good and much of it dealt with the German occupation of the Channel Islands. There was little hint of what would have happened in our capital city. The producers should have taken a look at Berlin in 1945. Had we put up much of a fight in the projected invasion of Britain in 1940, London might well have looked like this.

Berlin was a terrifying sight. The debris of battle was still to be seen everywhere. Lorries and tanks stood rusted where they had come to a halt across the roads. Not a tree was standing in the Tiergarten. Single walls and mounds of bricks were all that remained of streets and avenues. Here and there were soldiers' hastily dug graves marked with crosses. Imagine St James's Park and the Mall without trees, Whitehall bombed flat with the skeleton of the House of Parliament in the distance. From the crashed girders of Victoria Station you would be able to see the windowless wreck of Buckingham Palace, the broken tower of Westminster Cathedral and half the Abbey lying on the ruins of St Margaret's. And, if Nelson's Column were still standing, you know what would be flying at the top. The Four Horsemen had not just passed over Berlin; they had galloped backwards and forwards until hardly one stone had been left upon another. If ever a city had sown the wind and reaped the whirlwind, it was Berlin. From this centre the orders had gone out for the enslavement of Europe. Here had been planned the destruction of Rotterdam and Warsaw to mention only two of the German masterpieces of annihilation. The bureaucrats of this city had organized the murder of millions of Jews with the same efficiency they would have devoted to the reorganization of the Post Office or the railways. Though one was almost stunned at this destruction of a great city, one could not help feeling that, if justice had ever been done, it had been done to Berlin.

Men and women, hungry-looking and shabbily dressed, shuffled about touting in the hope of getting a few cigarettes. Allied soldiers in many different uniforms strolled over the rubble sightseeing and souvenir hunting. The focal point for tourists was of course Hitler's Chancellery, then a ruin.

The marble-topped table in Hitler's own room had been smashed to pieces. I still have a fragment as a paperweight. Papers and all manner of rubbish was strewn on the floor. Russian guards, mainly little Mongolian troops, patrolled the building. These neat, tough little men kept their fingers on the trigger all the time. There was no arguing with people like that, especially as I do not speak a word of Outer Mongolian, so I kept clear of them – until the incident of Hitler's toilet-roll holder. This was one of the spoils of war which, in a rash moment I had promised to procure for my C.O. in England. On retrospect this sounds rather childish but I was a lot younger then. I had been joined by another officer of my unit and we went into

Hitler's W.C., which adjoined his room. We found that the chromium-plated holder was sealed in with white tiles! To have come all this way and to retire without the precious relic was unthinkable, so we started to hack out the tiles with a pen knife. While we were engaged on the task, a rough-looking Russian guard came up. Expecting to be shot at any moment, I pointed to my cap and said "English aeroplane", the only two words I know in Russian apart from *Nyet*. I fervently hoped that he would interpret my words as "Royal Air Force". He merely thought we were mad and, probably not wishing to provoke us to further and more dangerous lunacies, began to help us to remove the object, he laughing the while. Once detached, I put the holder under my arm and took out my cigarette case, in which there were mercifully two cigarettes. I gave him one and we parted the best of friends. In due course the toilet-roll holder was despatched to London, possibly in the diplomatic bag.

In one part of the Chancellery a great hole had been made in the floor, leaving a yawning chasm, which no one had bothered to cover or fence round. As we walked through the various rooms everything had been smashed. Pictures had often been torn from the walls, papers were scattered all over the floors, any portraits had had the eyes shot out — a frequent sight in houses in the fighting zones — and many rooms had been used as public lavatories and were filled with buzzing flies. In view of the present craze for collecting Nazi relics, one could have made a fortune today by picking up the various insignia of the Nazi Party strewn everywhere. I contented myself with two of Hitler's gilt-bronze door handles and three prints of classical Greek subjects, coloured by hand, which were unaccountably lying in the debris. In all my journeying in Germany I could have collected a sackful of Iron Crosses.

In the centre of Berlin no building remained undamaged. The spire of the Gedächtnis Kirche still stood, though badly twisted and broken. Standing up among flattened buildings were the great solid Flak towers, aerial photographs of which had puzzled us during the war. They defied several of our attempts to blow them up, much to the amusement of the Berliners. The Russians had already erected a monument on which stood the first tank to break into Berlin. Later they were to build a more permanent memorial not far from the Brandenburg Gate. This construction went on day and night for a long time behind high wooden walls. The Russians were very touchy about anyone photographing their troops, especially if they were engaged in barter. I was about to take a picture of some Russian soldiers negotiating with an old German woman for a petticoat which I would not have used for a duster. Such things were obviously in short supply back home in Russia. A Russian major came up and tapped me rather menacingly on the shoulder. I thought it best not to argue and made off.

I had very much wanted to explore the famous Bunker, but I was informed that a visitor only the day before had accidentally kicked a hand grenade hidden in the rubbish on the floor. Having survived five years of war, I had no wish to die like Hitler in the Bunker, so I stayed upstairs. However, I had a talk with a woman who told me that she did the washing for the Bunker staff and she showed me the spot where the bodies of Hitler and Eva Braun had been burned. There were still doubts at that time about what had exactly happened to the Nazi leaders and Hugh Trevor-Roper had come out to investigate and establish the facts. The washerwoman had no such doubts. She was there, she said.

I spent one day at the Berlin Yacht Club at the Tegelsee, one of the large lakes near Berlin. There we went for a sail with the secretary, who considered himself amply rewarded with a few cigarettes and the remains of our sandwiches.

I returned several times to Berlin. This was the first horrifying impression. All the might which had threatened us and indeed all the world for five years was now a squalid ruin haunted by shabby, undernourished Germans trying to sell the last rags of their possessions for a few cigarettes.

In some parts of Germany people seemed at least to have been fed. These gaunt spectres in Berlin had clearly been through Hell. I could imagine what it was like only a few months before, when the little woman test pilot, Hanna Reitsch, had landed a small aircraft in the centre of the city through the fire of Russian A.A. guns, with General Ritter von Greim crouched behind her in the tiny cockpit. It must have been like landing in the lake of fire of Dante's Inferno. After years of our air bombardment, Russian guns had pulverized the city before it had finally become a fiercely contested battlefield in which boys of sixteen held out to the last. These people wandering about had somehow lived and survived while the city blazed and exploded, while traitors were summarily hanged on lamp posts and the dead defenders were hurriedly buried in front gardens. Meanwhile the maniacs in the Bunker below the Chancellery had played out their last grotesque charades in their little box-like rooms; Hitler screaming orders to non-existent armies and Goebbels methodically arranging the murder of his children.

Looking round, it seemed that the ruins could never be cleared, that these tanks and lorries would remain for ever in this moon landscape. One felt this was a just retribution. The people who had rained fire and murder from one end of Europe to the other, who had rendered millions homeless had now experienced the invasion of the Mongolian hordes and were homeless themselves.

It was on a subsequent visit to Berlin that I ventured into the Russian sector in my car and got out to have a look round the Silesian Station. There were pitiful groups of women and children, pale and hungry, on the platforms, groups of despair such as I had seen at the Gare d'Orléans in 1940. These Germans were the lucky ones. They had come by train. There were many thousands then tramping the roads westwards towards Berlin, moving from one lot of ruins to another.

One could go on philosophizing among the ruins of Berlin, about the Nazis and just retribution or one could look back dispassionately a quarter of a century or more later with Michael Howard on TV at the grand strategy of the war from a historian's distance, but today Mrs Smith and her children in an air-raid shelter in Clapham or, for that matter, Frau Schmidt and *her* children in a similar shelter in Köpenick are forgotten, like all the other lessons of history.

XXIV

Soon after my arrival in Lübbecke, I was moved to Bad Salzuflen, a little spa town in Lippe. It was full of doctors' consulting rooms and boarding houses. There was a central pump room, which was converted into the Bath Club for officers. It was surrounded with gardens where high hedges were sprayed with water. This was supposed to humidify the air for sufferers from respiratory diseases. Every house in Bad Salzuflen was well supplied with health literature, always including Professor Someone's "Neue Heilmethode" (New Health Cure) and the whole place was a hypochondriac's dream. Our occupation certainly drove the hypochondriacs out, since I observed no one taking the cure while I was there. It was at least a good place for dysentery. I got mine there.

As in Lübbecke, a whole section of the town had been taken over by the military and the Control Commission. Our offices were in a house which had been used for consulting rooms. The doors were all padded as in a lunatic asylum. I shared a house with one or two senior officers and we kept some of the rooms available for visiting dignitaries from London. Our secretaries lived in a kind of ladies' seminary in another larger house. As I have mentioned before, the Germans had to vacate their homes with only as much luggage as they could carry. That meant that our houses were reasonably well furnished, but once we had settled in, we found that one house might be short of household articles which were plentiful in another. So an enormous exchange and mart began. One house, for instance, might need four more dining room chairs for which the occupiers would swap a piano. Someone else required a bookcase and was prepared to give up a settee. By the time we were there a few weeks, scarcely any of the houses contained their original furnishings intact. God only knows how the inhabitants recovered their belongings after we left. Still, we did take care of the furniture and other household equipment and I feel sure the inhabitants of Bad Salzuflen found little missing once they got their goods and chattels finally sorted out.

Cigarettes remained the most important commodity and in fact the real currency of the country. I had my watch repaired and the cost was three cigarettes, negotiated by one of our men. An officer would have given twenty and cheap at that, but it would have spoilt the market. A carpenter made my wife a fine sewing box for ten and he thought he had done well. A black market in food flourished. While most Germans were on short commons and limited to a tasteless fluid which passed for beer, there were places where one could get a good steak and the right kind of drink.

I went frequently to Hamburg during my stay in Germany. In the other cities I had visited I thought I had seen the ultimate in destruction by bombing but Hamburg was to surpass them all. At times I put up at the Atlantic in the centre of the town. It had miraculously survived to serve as a hotel for officers. Otherwise I stayed at a house in Blankenese outside Hamburg on the banks of the Elbe. This had obviously been the home of a highly cultivated family of artists, to judge by the pictures and books in the house. There was a most beautiful spiral staircase and a circular dining room, which was decorated with a continuing seascape and landscape all round. Coming there from the ruins of Hamburg, it was scarcely credible that this island of civilization could exist so close to a city which seemed to have been completely destroyed.

One could drive out from the centre of Hamburg along the road to Bergedorf for twenty minutes and see nothing but ruins. Every street leading off to right or left on the main road was either bombed flat or burnt out. One heard all manner of horror stories of the great fire storm raid on the city. Most of the victims had been roasted alive in the cellars as the fire raced across the streets, turning the shelters into ovens. It was said that badly burned people who had jumped into the Alster lakes in the centre had had to be finished off with the revolver by officials in boats. The Burgomaster maintained that the death figure was not far from a hundred thousand.

On one drive, I passed a synagogue which had been bombed. All around lay great heaps of fragments of tombstones inscribed in Hebrew. I thought that the Germans would have long ago destroyed such a building and its cemetery, but it had been left to us to complete the job.

One of my tasks in Germany was to procure a copy of a certain

German scientific work, which was needed in London and which had not been available during the war. I went through university libraries in Berlin, Göttingen, Frankfurt and other towns before I discovered that there was a copy in the library of the Physikalisch-Technische Reichsanstalt of the University of Hamburg. I asked the appropriate professor, a delightful old character, for the book. He replied that it was out on loan. We were used to all kinds of evasions, so I gave him three days over the week-end to get it. I did not feel happy at having to menace such a distinguished figure, especially as he was half dead with cold and wrapped up in blankets. The first winter of the occupation was a severe one and shortage of fuel made life a misery for all of us. When I called again, he handed me the book. I was so pleased at having succeeded at last in my quest that I asked what I could do in return. He said he would like some coal, as the whole place was unheated. The students were unable to work owing to the cold. As they could well have been working on the construction of an atomic bomb – we had not yet found out how advanced Germany was at that time – I remained unmoved. Even a wealthy banker friend, who was one of my 'sources', used to bring a bag of peat into Hamburg every day to warm his enormous office. "Ask me for diamonds or gold bars, but not coal!" I replied. Everyone needed coal. It was clear that he himself would not survive very long that winter, so I told him despairingly that I would do what I could.

I went to the branch of the Control Commission dealing with fuel and told them a story about the importance of the help I had received from the old professor. I had no hope of getting any coal, but to my surprise they delivered twenty tons in the following few days. I wondered whom I was depriving and felt very guilty at my eloquence in getting blood out of a stone, but at least I had done someone a good turn. When I went back to see the old man, he was pitiful in his gratitude. He insisted on hobbling along, draped in blankets, to see me off at the main entrance. There on the steps of the institute, he stopped and made a speech beginning, "I personally and in the name of the whole Institute thank you, Herr Oberst, most deeply, sincerely –" and so he went on in typical German fashion. I got away as soon as I could, hoping that there would never be an enquiry into my fiddling twenty tons of coal which were probably more urgently needed elsewhere. So much for my small contribution to science.

Much of my work was in scientific and technical intelligence and on another occasion in Hamburg I had to call on a scientific establishment engaged in the manufacture of sera against certain diseases. Towards the end of my visit, it was mentioned that there was one department I had not seen – the section dealing with typhus. Would I care to make an inspection? I showed little enthusiasm but I felt I could not let these Germans see that I was scared. "Sie haben kein' Angst?" (You're not afraid?) said the doctor, leading me upstairs. "Not at all!" said I bravely, feeling like Sidney Carton mounting the steps of the guillotine and telling myself that it was plain lunacy to have survived the war only to die of typhus in the ruins of Hamburg. Did not Arnold Bennett die of typhus or typhoid through drinking water in Paris? If it was as easy as that, I was a dead man already. Why don't I admit that I am a coward or that I have a train to catch?

In a room upstairs we found three very pretty girls in white coats. Even they could not take my mind off imminent death. They were attending to stacks of small cages covering one whole side of the room. In these cages were thousands of mice, supposedly all suffering from typhus. On the other side of the room were a number of horizontal glass cases containing eggs, into which the dreaded disease was injected for incubation. I made every pretence to appear interested and I asked the doctor if the girls were immune. "Oh yes," said he, "they are inoculated regularly." That's all very fine, I thought, I'm not, and I could drop down dead with typhus at any moment for all they care. In fact, being Germans, they might even be pleased to see the invading British officer in the same situation as those mice. I got out of that room as soon as I decently could and the doctor then kindly invited me to tea with his family who lived on the premises. I accepted rather reluctantly, wondering if the cups were properly sterilized. You never know when you live in a kind of disease factory.

At tea, the doctor's little boy asked me if I would like to see his pets. "Indeed I would!" I replied, for I am very fond of children, much more than grown-ups. Then he produced a very large glass jar half filled with sawdust, on which two white mice were scampering! The brothers of those mice upstairs? I asked nervously if they were not afraid of infection and they all laughed. "Of course not!" They were all inoculated, while I was liable to collapse with typhus at any minute. When I got back to Bad Salzuflen, I was glad for once that half the library was made up of medical books. I looked up typhus and found that the incubation period is just under three weeks and that the symptoms are most unpleasant. During the ensuing three weeks I persuaded myself that I had them all and it was only at the end of the incubation period that I came to the conclusion that I had not contracted typhus.

In Hamburg I had occasion to visit the Blohm and Voss shipyards where the submarines were built and which were so often the target of our bombers. There on the stocks were six large submarines entirely undamaged despite the obvious results of bombing in the vicinity. It seemed a miracle that the principal objectives of our bombing had remained untouched. As they were high on land, one had to climb a long ladder to get into the conning tower and then descend another ladder to get down inside. I left it to my assistant to make an inspection. I have a horror of enclosed spaces like coalmines and the interiors of submarines.

Another target which survived the bombing were the U-boat pens on the opposite bank of the Elbe from Blankenese but near Hamburg. Protected by a great depth of solid concrete, these pens were impenetrable and it was no small task to destroy them. I was at Blankenese when they were blown up. Though we were a good way down the river, we could see the pens through field glasses from our river terrace. At the count down, one saw a red glow gradually splitting the enormous mass of concrete horizontally and then later came the boom of the explosion. We unwisely stayed on the terrace, thinking it was all over, until debris began to rain down on us even at that distance. It was an impressive spectacle and successful, unlike our desperate attempts on the Flak towers in Berlin, which remained immovable. Not long ago, I saw a Flak tower in the centre of Vienna, which no one seems anxious to destroy.

The first winter was one of misery for us all, occupiers and occupied. It was bitterly cold and we often had to call off journeys on account of the icy roads. It was a difficult time for the Control Commission. Heating, lighting, water and food were priorities apart from the denazification problems in dealing with local government officials. Sheep had to be separated from goats. Countless "Fragebogen" (questionnaires) had to be filled in with all the usual language difficulties. Not many of the Control Commission had a sound knowledge of German and many Germans were quick to take advantage of this. The quality of the Control Commission staffs varied. There were many who were able and dedicated but I had the impression — and this is purely a personal opinion — that some of the lower ranks were not up to the job of administering an occupied country. Recruitment could not have been easy and the authorities must have had to scrape the bottom of the barrel here and there. Most people wanted to get back to Britain after the war and begin life again. Few wanted to live in a devastated country away from their families. Thus it was by no means our best who went forth to govern Germany. I found one senior police official who knew no German and whose subordinates made rude remarks in his presence without realizing that the visiting R.A.F. officer understood what they were saying. I learned that he had been a village constable. Still, they did their best and, together with the industry of the German character, managed slowly to rebuild some kind of order and avoid the anarchy, which could have broken out as it did after the 1914 war.

My modest house in Bad Salzuflen was shared first with a senior S.O.E. brigadier and then with a colonel who had been a master at Eton, both stimulating companions to live with. Among our guests from various branches of Intelligence were the late Airey Neave, a man of great charm and ability, to whom I owed my assignment to Nuremberg, the redoubtable Professor Norman, oddly disguised in a wing commander's battle-dress, and Kim Philby, who wore no uniform. I found Philby a very pleasant and forceful character, as indeed he must have been to have fooled us all for so long. He could drink and still keep his head. His speech impediment could be embarrassing but it could have proved an advantage as it gave him at times a good ten seconds to think up an answer. Another guest was Christopher Robin's cousin, which added an odd note to the strange assortment gathered in our exclusive little club.

Our domestic staff consisted of a demobilized German soldier and Anneliese, the maid, who were supervised by a British gunner. Among many other duties they had to bring in the lamps when the electric light failed just as we sat down to dinner. We attributed this to sabotage at the power station but no one did anything about it. S.S. officers dining in England would have solved the problem with a few bullets but we dined in the hissing glare of the Tilley lamps.

XXV

One of my more interesting expeditions was to the university town of Göttingen. As part of the old kingdom of Hanover with many links with our own royal house, Göttingen might have been expected to give a warmer welcome to the occupying forces than other German towns. Yet the natives were far from friendly and in fact it was the only place I visited where it was made very clear that we were not wanted.

It was strange to find monuments to kings of England and Captain Cook's original collection of artefacts from the South Seas, which had been a gift of George III, in this hostile atmosphere. I went to see this collection in the museum, as it is of particular interest in showing the arts of a Pacific culture before the results of what Alan Moorehead called the fatal impact had taken effect.

This visit was especially memorable for it was in Göttingen that I had a chance of talking to the great physicists, Otto Hahn and Werner Heisenberg. I went to see them in the temporary home we had given them before their removal to England. I took them a few tins of sardines, which seemed a modest offering to two great scientists, one of whom had discovered nuclear fission. Hahn was horrified when he realized that his discovery had led to Hiroshima. Years later, when I was serving at H.M. Embassy in Berne, I met Hahn again when he came to lecture there. I have always had the greatest admiration for him and I was glad on that occasion to be able to present my son, then a student, to such a distinguished man.

While I was in Göttingen, I heard that Mozart's *Il Seraglio* was being played at the Opera House. Despite the anti-British feeling I decided to go. I was surprised to find that I was the only one in uniform in the whole audience, so I sat there in the middle of the front row of the circle, hoping not to be noticed. At one point in the performance, one of the two female captives in the harem – I cannot remember which one – stepped forward very deliberately and declaimed, "Ach, wie schwer ist es unter der Fremdenherrschaft zu leiden!" (Ah, how hard it is to suffer under the foreigner's rule!) The appropriateness of these words in the first year of our occupation was not lost on the audience, which broke into spontaneous applause. Many turned round to see how the British officer was taking it and were surprised to see that I too was clapping.

However, I was not sorry to leave Göttingen and soon after I was in Berlin again. This time one of my chores was to look round the Japanese and Italian embassies, both of which had been damaged and partly looted. Every room in both buildings was littered ankle-deep in books and papers. At that time I had with me a Dutch intelligence officer, Colonel Michels, who was also a professor of physics in the University of Amsterdam. In a heap of rubbish in one room of the Japanese embassy, we came upon a fine Samurai sword. Having come across it simultaneously, we had to toss for it and I won. There was one other souvenir there which I would have liked to take away and that was an enormous bronze figure, which had stood at the top of a flight of marble stairs. Unfortunately it weighed several tons. It had been thrown down and it lay head downwards on the broken stairs. On the floor in one large room a great crystal chandelier lay smashed to pieces. In most of the rooms were the usual stacks of invitation cards and photographs of Japanese diplomats shaking hands with the Party bosses. The most surprising find of all was a large consignment of forged Chinese passports.

A tour round the Italian embassy produced a cross of the Order of the Crown of Italy with its relative certificate not yet filled in and a large stock of wedding rings. They were of white metal and of all sizes. It will be remembered that one of Mussolini's confidence tricks had been to persuade the women of Italy to give up their gold wedding rings to pay for the war in Ethiopia. In exchange they received one of these trumpery substitutes inscribed "For King and Country" on the inside. Those which I found were to be doled out to expatriate Italian women silly enough to give up their most treasured possession to satisfy the ambitions of this mountebank. Here again were stocks of photographs, many of Hitler and Mussolini together, some of them taken after the Skorzeny rescue when Mussolini looked twenty years older.

The Gestapo H.Q. in the Prinz Albrechtstrasse was next on my sightseeing list. My secretary was anxious to see the place and I allowed her to come with me. The building was locked up so I decided to break in after dark. We took a torch and found a policeman who looked as if he needed a good meal. For ten cigarettes — a princely bribe then — he helped us to get in at the back and agreed to keep cave while we were inside. We went down into some corridors lined with tiny cells, each with a stout door. A more sinister and nauseating place I cannot imagine. Suddenly in the light of the torch I saw what looked like a long black carpet extending along one of the passages. When we got closer it proved to be not a carpet but a hole and it seemed to have no bottom. Happily we had not walked into it. There must have been some kind of flooring which could be removed for some nasty purpose. The floors of the various rooms were littered with lists of prisoners and papers covering concentration camp transfers, all neatly filled in and signed as if it were the Post Office Savings Bank. Never have I been more glad to get out of a building as I was to leave that evil institution. Before I left, I brought out a few copies of a book of instructions issued for the invasion of Britain and containing lists of those to be arrested. My name was not to be found anywhere. Sometimes it pays to be obscure.

It was on my visit to Berlin with Colonel Michels that I had my first encounter with Russian troops in the mass. We were three-quarters of the way up the autobahn to Berlin when our radiator began to give trouble. We were clearly not going to make Berlin without some water. The autobahn to Berlin is not remarkable for the beauty of its scenery. It is just flat plain on either side. However, I saw what looked like a village on the horizon to the south, so we decided to break all the rules and drive off the road. As we approached the village, Russian soldiers began to surround the car and finally we were in the village with what seemed half the Russian army round us. No one spoke German or French and we knew no Russian. An officer came up and we made signs, pointing to the radiator and pretending to drink. Meanwhile soldiers kept coming up and shaking hands with us. One man in particular kept promenading in front of us to show us his medals, on which we congratulated him with handshakes and pats on the back, wondering meanwhile if we were going to be shot or imprisoned. Our car was a great attraction. They did not see many western cars in that village. Finally it dawned on them what we wanted. With one accord the whole Russian army turned round and shouted "Natasha!", upon which a plump Russian girl appeared and was told to go and get some water. Off she went to the pump while we handed round cigarettes. They patched our radiator, filled us up and to our great relief let us go.

The Russians were a curious mixture of saturnine ferocity and childish good humour and I could well imagine they were first-class soldiers. I was coming down the autobahn on another occasion with another officer in a car packed with documents of rather a secret nature which we had obtained in Berlin. We were hoping that we would have no trouble on the autobahn in the Russian zone or at Helmstedt on the way out. All went well till we were two hours out of Berlin, when we were overtaken by a Russian soldier on a motorcycle. He signalled us to stop and we pulled over to the side of the road. There were just the three of us with our driver and nothing else in sight in any direction. Again the language barrier. We did not know if he wanted to seize our documents, arrest us or just pass the time of day as a comrade in arms against Hitler. Had we been Germans, we could have shot him, pushed him and his motorcycle in the ditch and driven on. So we tried the cigarette and handshake technique and grinned at one another while we tried to understand what he wanted.

We then noticed that it was not a Russian motorcycle and it then dawned on us that he had pinched it somewhere and was simply showing off. So we encouraged him by signs to put it through its paces and let us see how he handled it. He did a few trial runs up and down the road, which all the time remained free of any other traffic. Finally we suggested that he should try a long run-up in the direction of Berlin, which he was glad to do. Surely he must be running out of petrol by now, we thought. Anyhow, as he almost disappeared in the other direction, we decided to clamber into the car again and get going. Our driver stepped on it and that was the last we saw of our Russian friend. At Helmstedt they ignored the parcels of documents altogether.

There was one encounter in Germany which stunned me completely and that was with a young German girl. I was about to leave Rothenburg ob der Taube with another officer to go to Würzburg. We had just walked round this lovely old town, which mercifully escaped the bombing. Just as we were getting into the car, this German girl came up and asked us if we could give her a lift to Würzburg. Usually we did not give lifts to Germans unless they were old or with children. This time we relented, though the girl was anything but attractive. She jumped in the back with the other officer and myself. "To the station!" she said to the driver in a commanding voice. I was too surprised to say anything. Arrived at the railway station, she got out and came back after a few minutes carrying an enormous cardboard suitcase and a large shopping bag. We put the suitcase in the boot and set off, she comfortably ensconced in the back with us. Within two minutes, she announced, "I'm hungry!" and proceeded to unpack her shopping bag, from which she extracted various packages of food. She then solemnly ate her way to Würzburg. Never in my life have I seen anyone pack so much food into a stomach. Not a word did she vouchsafe. She did not offer to share the feast. She just ate and ate.

As we came in sight of the Würzburg bridge with its rows of statues along the parapet, she crammed the last scraps of food into her mouth, assembled her belongings and called to the driver to pull up and get her suitcase out of the boot. She seized it and ran off with it, heavy as it was, just in time to catch a bus leaving the stop by the bridge. Not a "Thank you", no "Goodbye", she just went. We sat stunned. We could not even laugh. That girl would have stopped the car of Juggernaut in its tracks. Sadly we set off for Frankfurt.

I often wonder what the Germans thought of *us*. At first they were not a little scared. Some thought us mad – or at least thought me mad – like the little boy at Ansbach. I had stopped my car outside the Schloss or Palace or whatever it is called. I took it to be the residence of the Margrave. The little boy came up and stared at my uniform. I told him why I was interested and asked him if he knew that a Queen of England had come from his part of Germany, Caroline of Ansbach, the wife of George II. He was politely interested and regarded me with some sympathy, the sympathy which is reserved for the slightly cracked. Perhaps I had got hold of the wrong Ansbach.

Then there was the attendant at the pay kiosk of the wrecked Frankfurt Zoo. "Sie müssen bezahlen!" (You must pay!) said he. I pointed out that he was in no position to use the auxiliary verb 'must' to a British officer – and paid. I've never seen a man more surprised. I had a better reception at Hagenbeck's Zoo near Hamburg. I was taken round what was left of it and I was shown a most remarkable exhibit which had escaped the bombing. It appears that they once had two large pythons there. One night they had engaged in a life and death struggle, which ended in a square shallow pool in their enclosure. Neither would relinquish its grasp on the other and they both drowned. They were found next morning literally in their death throes. The director then had the idea of emptying the pool and filling it with plaster to take a cast of the two intertwined reptiles. This was later cast in bronze to be kept as a permanent memorial to two pythons who would not give up.

No account of the occupation of Germany would be complete without introducing the word 'swanning'. It was in the first two years that 'swan' came into general use both as a noun and a verb. I know nothing of the etymology of the word. I had never heard it before, so I suppose it was born of the occupation. To go off on a swan or to go swanning could be interpreted in various ways. It could mean a long week-end away from one's normal job, possibly well deserved, but the usual significance suggested something illicit. One invented an official excuse to go down to Brussels. One's colleagues knew very well that it did not matter a damn whether one went to Brussels or not but it was good for a few days' holiday or some night-clubbing. The occupying forces generally had transport and drivers at their disposal. While Germans had to remain static or rely on the few overcrowded trains, we could take off for Berlin or Hamburg when we liked. It was this mobility which encouraged swanning on a grand scale. If you could take a girl with you on a swan, so much the better. If you called on an official who was not available, the only conclusion you could reach was that he was away on a swan. An intelligence officer's job needed no excuse for a swan. One had to 'swan around' to get information. It came to the point that even genuine journeys were interpreted as swans.

Yet, despite the swanning, fratting and fiddling, a tremendous amount of work was done in getting the Germans on their feet again. The Control Commission brought order out of chaos and the industrious character of the Germans did the rest. At a time when we had decided to let willow herb flourish for twenty years on bombed sites in London – a fig tree grew to full maturity from a cellar near Aldersgate Station – the Germans suddenly decided to clear up. In most of the bombed cities of Germany teams of women of all ages began to appear, armed with trowels and brushes. Every brick was picked up, cleaned of mortar, carefully brushed and neatly stacked. It was not a good idea for a R.A.F. car to stop and view these proceedings. Some of the viragos thus employed were inclined to menace one with a newly cleaned brick. Even in the winter this work went on, the women wearing thick shawls and heavy gloves.

This is far from the whole story of the occupation of Germany. In these chapters I have tried to give some personal impressions and to convey some idea of what defeat and occupation mean to a people – whether it is France or Germany. I have written in the first part of this book of the frightening experience of finding oneself alone in an abandoned town. I remember Rheims with its hungry dogs and Amiens as I drove through the empty echoing streets at night in 1940. In our organized society of today, we do not realize how near we live to the edge of the abyss. We seldom think of what happens when law and order break down. In the San Francisco earthquake of 1906, one would have thought that people would be drawn together in adversity. Not a bit of it. They started to loot the liquor shops. The soldiers were called in to control the population at the end of a gun. When I lived in Brussels a few years ago, a great fire destroyed the Innovation department store and over four hundred people perished in the first five minutes of the blaze. Yet among the few who got out was one man with a camera, which he had snatched from the counter near the door. Did he think of turning round to save a child? In one minute all the civilization had dropped off. In France when everything broke down in 1940 and in the mad rush to an unknown destination, you siphoned the petrol from your neighbour's car while he slept. We were soon back to the jungle.

So in Germany. In 1945 everything had broken down too and I had this same feeling of terror in those ghost towns and cities where people crept among the ruins trying to find their way back to life again. The present generation in Germany knows nothing of all this any more than our own young people remember sirens and A.R.P. and ration books and the men and women who never came home again. Perhaps it is just as well.

Epilogue

Silent witness at Nuremberg

Epilogue in Nuremberg

In March 1946 I had the good fortune to be invited to Nuremberg by Mr Justice Robert H. Jackson, the principal American prosecutor, to be present at the trial of the Major War Criminals. The purpose of my visit was to talk to Albert Speer, Hitler's Minister for Armaments and War Production. For the occasion I was raised very temporarily to the rank of V.I.P., since only persons of that eminence could stay at the Grand Hotel.

Before going to the Court House, I took a walk through the bomb-damaged town to look at what was left of Dürer's house. Fortunately it was not beyond repair. I thought of some of the other great men Germany has produced and wondered how this gifted nation could have handed itself over to the gang of thugs whose trial I was about to witness.

When I arrived at the Court House, sentries presented arms as I went in. They were drawn in turn from each of the occupying powers and vied with one another on their smart turn-out. Inside, security was on the James Bond scale. Though I was in R.A.F. uniform, I was challenged again and again before reaching the courtroom.

It is difficult to describe my feelings on first seeing the two rows of prisoners. Since 1939 we had lived under the threat of annihilation at the hands of this mob. Here they were now, safely caged and disarmed, and I could examine them at my leisure. In the front row at one end of the dock lolled the nonchalant Goering, apparently at his ease. Quite clearly the only one. His uniform jacket, devoid of orders or medals, hung loosely on his much reduced frame. He looked almost handsome after some of the photographs I had seen of him when he was playing the Roman emperor. Next to him sat the mad Hess, brows knit and arms folded, staring straight before him. On the other side was Ribbentrop, tired, worn-out and obviously very nervous. Then came stuffed-shirt Keitel in uniform. I do not think he could have been very happy to have the sinister Kaltenbrunner as his neighbour. His horse face and dead-pan look came straight out of a horror film. Rosenberg, Frank and Frick followed, alike in their mediocrity. There was an empty chair next to Frick. The monstrous Streicher was indisposed while I was there and I was spared the sight of him. At the end sat the nondescript Funk with the wily Schacht. Ley, another missing figure, had committed suicide.

In the back row behind Goering sat the admirals, Doenitz and Raeder, the youthful Schirach, Sauckel, who looked as ugly as his name, Jodl in uniform and next to him the old fox, von Papen. He really did look like a cornered fox. Seyss-Inquart, Speer, von Neurath and Fritzsche completed the back row. Behind them stood seven "Snowdrops", smart American service men in their white steel helmets. More "Snowdrops", armed with revolvers, stood at the side of the dock.

Many of the prisoners wore very dark sun-glasses. I cannot think why, unless they wanted to hide behind them. The judges, American, British, French and Russian, did not wear such glasses. Nor did anyone else in the court. It was the first thing which struck me. One felt like calling upon them to unmask and look the world in the face. In front of the dock sat the counsel, one for each prisoner, and on their right as they faced the judges was the prosecutor's lectern. Behind glass cages opposite sat the interpreters, whose voices were relayed to the headphones which most of us wore. Translation was slow, as the red light on each microphone would come on warning the speaker to keep his speed down.

I sat in the low gallery with four press buttons on the arm of my chair so that I could select which language I wanted. The whole atmosphere was intensely dramatic. We all knew that we were assisting at a trial which was unique in history, a trial which was the last act of a drama of pity and terror such as the world had never seen and at a scene of retribution for crimes the horror of which we had not yet grasped despite the evidence which was presented to us. And here, within a few feet of us, was this undistinguished band of criminals who had wielded power which no other ruler in history had ever had and who had done these things.

It was hardly to be expected that any of them would be looking their best after months in prison, but there were few who had any air of distinction or even intelligence. Even Landru put up a better show than this. The soldiers tried to look self-important, the sailors looked sulky, Ribbentrop appeared to be about to burst into tears. Speer was pensive but at least looked intelligent. Schacht never missed a point. As to the rest they were a dreary lot of nonentities. Again and again I had the thought – how had the German people allowed themselves to be ruled by this gang?

In the few days I was there, Ribbentrop was cross-examined by David Maxwell-Fyfe. There was some delay in getting Ribbentrop into the witness box. His counsel was raising some technical objection about a document which had not been produced. Finally, Lord Lawrence, the British judge, said, "Are you or are you not going to call your witness?" Counsel signified vaguely that he was, "Then call him!" snapped Lawrence. Ribbentrop literally shambled to the witness box, clutching his papers, and began a statement which I listened to in German. He began by saying when and where he was born, adding that it was near to France, a country which he came to admire. So the dreary preamble went on till he was called upon to face Maxwell-Fyfe's questions. It was a pitiful performance for a man noted for his duplicity and cunning. Maxwell-Fyfe led him along with encouraging questions with Ribbentrop almost eagerly agreeing. Then, when he had got several admissions from the wretched witness, came the big question to which there was no answer. Ribbentrop was spitted neatly on Maxwell-Fyfe's rapier. I might have fallen for it myself. Maxwell-Fyfe seemed so kind and understanding. But only once. I would have been much more cautious next time. Yet Maxwell-Fyfe brought off the trick again and again till Ribbentrop was reduced to a floundering heap. One almost felt sorry for him. When he returned to the dock he was close to tears. Goering did not attempt to conceal his contempt. It was Ribbentrop who was the first to face the hangman when the time came for the bill to be paid.

One could not help feeling that one was watching a play on the stage rather than a trial in a criminal court. Yet all our acts, all our efforts, all our skills, however modest, over the past five years had been directed to bringing about this reality. How many more were there who deserved far more than we did to sit there and see justice done at last, how many who had contributed more than we had and who had striven and not survived to see the world freed from these monsters? All around were the ghosts of the victims, the millions who had died in the camps, the frozen corpses in front of Stalingrad, the drowned sailors of the *Bismarck* – and of the *Hood*, the dead men strewn along the North African coast and all those who had died from

Normandy to the Elbe. Outside in Europe and still alive were the millions of Displaced Persons, if one may use such a dry, legal expression, most of whom would never see their homes again.

And here in the dock sat the erstwhile lords of creation, hiding behind their sun-glasses and busying themselves with endless files and lawyers' quibbles. Not long ago, they held Europe from Norway to the Volga, from the White Sea to the Black Sea. I knew from captured documents what they had intended to do to us if they could only have followed us across the Channel in 1940. It was all planned and printed. Had I not brought out six copies of the book from the Gestapo prison in the Prinz Albrechtstrasse in Berlin? They sat there like lambs now but how long since they were ravening wolves?

We had let this happen. Surely at some point we could have stopped it. The German people could have stopped it. Perhaps a gale of laughter could have shut up for good the preposterous little man in the shabby raincoat. Ridicule is the best cure for would-be dictators. Yet they had allowed this vengeful little hysteric to lead them here to the dock at Nuremberg. It was a bewildering thought. I could not lay claim to any heroic exploits since 1939. I had just done my job and kept out of trouble, but I had been in a position on my roving commission to see more than many others how narrowly we had missed sharing the fate of the other victims. I had seen the Nazis going from triumph to triumph, the humiliation of France, the destruction of European civilization, the sweep of the conquering armies to the gates of Moscow and Cairo; and finally I had seen the ashes of the Götterdämmerung in the Chancellery in Berlin. And all that was left of the Thousand Year Reich was this bunch of mediocrities in the dock. Well might the Germans write on the walls of their ruined buildings, "It took Hitler twelve years to achieve this!"

In the evenings I talked to Speer. He sat there in a rather worn suit. He was not allowed to wear a tie or shoelaces. That was a precaution since Ley committed suicide. And he was allowed only one blunt implement to eat his supper. The first evening we had his lawyer, Hans Flächsner, present and of course the inevitable 'Snowdrop'. I suggested that it was not really necessary to have the lawyer there and on the second evening he came alone, but still under guard of course. He was a pleasant cultivated man and I must admit I enjoyed our talks. Nothing much of any intelligence value came from him. There was a little mutual leg-pulling about wasted bombing on both sides, as I have already mentioned. He was obviously a better type than most of the others in the dock. Perhaps for that reason he was one of the most dangerous.

Speer was a little man at the beginning caught up in great events. He was a newly fledged architect like thousands of others when he was taken up by Hitler. As time went on a tremendous prospect was opened up for him. He was to be the architect, the practical architect of the Thousand Year Reich. Berlin was to be re-built. The work of Baron Haussmann was to be a side-show in comparison. Gigantic buildings, mile-long avenues, triumphal arches, enormous sports stadia and all the other ambitions of the megalomaniac's dream — Speer was to be the man to realize them in marble and granite to last a thousand years. Most of them never got beyond the plaster model stage. Fascinated at an impressionable age by Hitler's personality and with such a career offered to him he was tempted. He also had ability. It was his genius which kept Germany afloat economically almost to the end. The Hitlers, Himmlers and Goebbels of this world have not the practical ability to repair a bicycle. But the Speers could forge the weapons for the hand of the dictator just as the financial genius of the Schachts could cook the books. As we know, Speer survived twenty years in prison, his intellect unimpaired. If a man of his outstanding ability could be dazzled and brainwashed by the Nazi lunacy — as he was until disillusionment with Hitler set in and he had a glimpse of the wrath to come — he could be that much more dangerous than the crazy Streicher or the mystic Hess.

Yet I cannot help feeling something akin to admiration for him. While everyone else sought exculpation in the old "Orders are orders" excuse, he took full responsibility for what he had done and he carries a heavy burden of guilt today. I have had some correspondence with him since his release and I am still puzzled that a man of his apparent sincerity could have landed himself up in the dock at Nuremberg. His *Memoirs* is in my opinion the most important book to come out of the Third Reich and his day-to-day account of the intrigues and manoeuvres of the Hitlerian Court is an impressive indictment of the whole system from the first rantings of *Mein Kampf* to the nightmare of the last days in the Bunker in Berlin and the retribution of the execution shed in Nuremberg.

By a curious coincidence years after the events described in my book, my son did part of his military service in Germany and was among the guards at Spandau.

Since 1946 many people have had misgivings about the strict

legality of the Nuremberg trials. What was the alternative in the spirit prevailing then? Let them loose to talk themselves through endless legal wrangles out of any responsibility and write articles for the Sunday papers or shoot them like mad dogs without trial? We have still not grasped the enormity of the evidence of the prosecution, not only evidence of what had been done but of what was intended for the world these men envisaged. The chronicle of horrors perpetrated is so vast that it is actually boring to read. Our minds cannot take it in. So when a dog with rabies is running among the children of the village, do we phone the R.S.P.C.A. for a dog psychologist? If we have any sense we get a gun or a strong cage.

Being the kind of people we are, we are appalled on retrospect at the destruction of Dresden and the fire storms of Hamburg. Then, it seemed right to repay every bomb on this country a hundredfold. Having seen Hamburg and other German cities immediately after the war, I realize how lightly we got off, though that is little consolation to those of us who lost everything in the raids on Britain. Now a generation has grown up which knows nothing of the dark days from 1939 to 1945 nor indeed of the heroism of our people in those times. Hitler moustaches and *Dad's Army* are still good for a laugh, but I cannot help thinking – What if *they* had won? as I did in Nuremberg in 1946.

Index

Index

18 12